# Thirty-Five Years In The Congo

## Congo

### A History of the Demonstrations of Divine Power In the Congo

by

WILLIAM B. WEAVER, M.A.

Foreword by
CHRISTIAN E. REDIGER, M.A.
*Secretary-Treasurer, Congo Inland Mission*

Published by
CONGO INLAND MISSION
1326 West 72nd Street
CHICAGO 36, ILLINOIS

# Dedicated To:

Those Who Have Labored
        for
The Redemption of the Bantu
        in
The Congo Inland Mission Field,
        and
To the Young People Who will yet Consecrate
Their Lives to Him in the Most Worth-while Service.

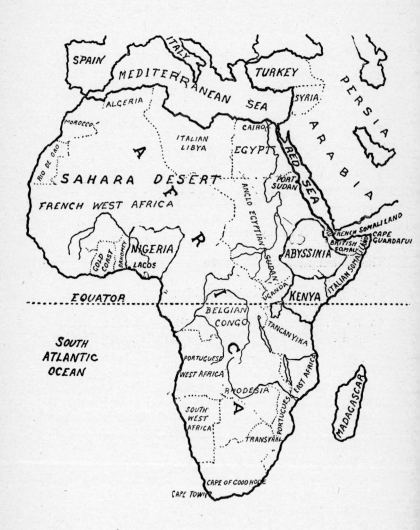

# Foreword

This book has been written and is being sent forth with a prayer that it might bring glory to Christ who has saved us, and that it might inspire young people to yield themselves to prepare for Missionary Service.

We kindly invite the reader to turn aside from the quiet and peace of his Christian home and atmosphere and by thought allow himself to meditate a bit upon the difficulties encountered in bringing the Gospel of Jesus Christ to the many dark brothers who waited so long in darkness, without God and without Hope. We believe you will be moved with inward delight, as you read also of the results and fruitage of this seed sowing in what was then known as "the open sore of the world."

The burden of this seed sowing was accepted from God by a group of people with increasing insistence, until about thirty-five years ago the Congo Inland Mission was formed. As you read on from page to page you will find that "No good thing has He withheld from His Own." God has blessed the sacrifice of love, answered many prayers, given strength and courage to face and endure many hardships, thousands have been saved, an effectual door has been opened wide. And yet, millions wait to be delivered from death. If you are willing to rescue them, not counting the cost and pain, may God show you, through prayer and by faith, your part in this "Go ye."

In order to make this testimony of Divine Power in the Congo, known to many, and realizing the value of publishing such a volume as this, the Congo Inland Mission Board asked Rev. William B. Weaver, of Danvers, Illinois (also a member of the Board) to gather statistics and information and write such an edition.

Rev. Weaver is eminently fitted to write just such a book as this, having majored in history while attending Indiana University during the spring and summer of 1914. He received his A. B. Degree from Goshen College, Goshen, Indiana of the same year. He became professor of history at this college in the Fall of 1914, which position he retained till 1920, when he began teaching Bible and Church History. In July 1922 he was called as pastor to the North Danvers Church, in the Central Conference of Mennonites, which pastorate he still holds. During this period of time Rev. Weaver has studied in Garrett Biblical Institute, majoring in Church History and received his Master's Degree in 1926 from Northwestern University. As a thesis for his Master's Degree Rev. Weaver compiled and wrote the book "History of the Central Conference of Mennonites."

The author's time and work was not given to praise workers, although they deserve tribute for their loyalty and co-operation, but to glorify the Lord who called them and blessed them so abundantly in their seed sowing to the Congolese. Also, as an encouragement to the Christian folk who stay at home to toil and support those whom the Lord has called to go. He who "clothed the grass of the field, feedeth the birds of the air" and "arrayed the lilies of the field," never forgets to reward even, "a cup of cold water."

Much valuable information is contained in this edition, giving the historical setting of the Congo Inland Missionary Work. Every Christian Worker and Home should be thoroughly familiar with it.

I hope and pray it will find a large circle of friends, to whom it will prove as much of a blessing as it has to me.

C. E. Rediger.

1326 West 72nd Street
Chicago 36, Illinois.

# Preface

The title of this book, "Thirty-five Years of Mission Work in the Congo," suggests the scope of the work and the years of history which are recorded. The history of missionary work in the Mennonite Church is of recent development. Although this religious group is over four hundred and fifty years old, their missionary history is only about fifty years. Because of persecution and their rural environment their missionary outlook has been of recent years. The Mennonites have been in America over two hundred and fifty years but much of this time was spent in the establishment of churches in United States and Canada.

What is true of the Mennonite Church in general is particularly true of the two co-operating groups which began missionary work in the Congo. Both Defenseless and Central Conference Churches came from the large group of Amish in America in the latter part of the nineteenth century so the missionary interests of these two groups began in about 1900.

The writer's interest in the writing of a history of the missionary work in the Congo began when he became a member of the Congo Inland Mission Board in 1927. This interest kept growing until in 1935 the Congo Inland Mission Board arranged for anniversary programs commemorating the twenty-five years of the mission work of the Congo Inland Mission. Rev. H. E. Bertsche of Gridley, Illinois and the writer were asked to write a booklet on our Twenty-five years in the Congo.

In 1938 the Mission Board definitely passed a resolution that a more complete history should be written
of our missionary work. The writer was asked to undertake this task. The years 1938-1944 were spent in the
collection of material particularly receiving material
from the field. In the October meeting of the Congo
Inland Mission Board of 1944 it was decided that this
history should be completed by April 1, 1945. The
writer, and his wife as stenographer, applied themselves arduously to this task and completed this history April 10, 1945.

One of the difficulties encountered in writing Mennonite history is the fact that the sources are very
meager; the Mennonites have not diligently recorded
the work which they have done. Part of it may be a
matter of modesty, but most of it is a lack of conviction as to the great importance of records and of the
great value of history. The writer was, however, fortunate in the fact that some of the earlier missionaries did faithfully record the work they were doing
on the field. In this Rev. L. B. Haigh must be given
particular credit for his informative annual reports of
the work on the field. On the other hand, some of our
earliest missionaries and members of the Board are
still with us and so much information could be received
through correspondence and private interviews. This
writing is rather a compendium of the history of our
mission work in the Congo. The writer was compel-
led because of the size of the book to give only an outline of what could have been written in detail. It is the
hope that others will take various phases of this history and continue the research in later years. The emphasis of this book is placed on the origins and the
early development of our mission work. The purpose
is to reveal principles and methods of work by a description of the actual activities on the field.

The author gratefully acknowledges his indebtedness to the many influences and factors that made possible the writing of this book. To give adequate acknowledgement to everyone who aided is impossible. The imperfections in the book belong to the author.

The writer, however, wishes to express his deepest appreciation to the Congo Inland Mission Board that decided to write such a history, to the missionaries who aided so much by the material they sent. Also acknowledgement is made with appreciation to the committee appointed by the Congo Inland Mission Board, Rev. Harry Bertsche, Rev. R. L. Hartzler and the Field Secretary, Rev. C. E. Rediger, who read either parts or all of the manuscript.

This history is sent forth with the hope and prayer that it might give information and inspiration to all who are so deeply interested in the redemption of the Bantu and the building of an African Christian Church.

**Wm. B. Weaver.**

May 22, 1945, Danvers, Illinois.

# Contents

# CHAPTER I

# Introduction

History is the record and interpretation of the life of man in his co-operation with others. This record may deal with various phases of man's life and achievements. History may thus record his interest in providing for his physical, mental, social, or spiritual needs. This historical survey is primarily interested in man's spiritual need. It is based upon records written by missionaries, members of the board and home church, and Christian leaders in the general field of missions.

It must always be borne in mind in the writing of history that we are dependent upon human witnesses and human interpretations which are always subject to fallibility; and, further, that the writer is human and therefore prone to be fallible in his interpretation. A conscientious effort shall be made, however, to be unprejudiced, fair and historical in the writing as far as possible. The writer is desirous that this history shall become a living, dynamic unfolding of a great spiritual enterprise in the Belgian Congo. His desire is further, as Mrs. Julia Lake Kellersberger said when she wrote Congo Crosses, "I want to be a pencil in the hands of God, that He might write this book."

It is very important to remember that in this historical survey our primary interest lies in the missionary activities of the church. It is an attempt to meet the spiritual needs of the natives in the Belgian Congo; while at the same time giving expression to the church's deepest convictions and interests, as they grow out of her fellowship with God through Jesus Christ. The church, of course, has other interests besides missions. It is interested in its policy, its doctrine, its worship, and the highest and most efficient spiritual life of its members. The life and work of our mission in the Congo will never rise higher than the life and work of the home church. In these critical days there is much emphasis placed upon present activities and programs, and post war plans,—this emphasis often at the expense of, interest in, and appreciation of the past. We become so absorbed in the "now" that we forget the "has been."

This is the first history written at some length, of our thirty-five years' work in the Congo. The question may be rightly asked as to the value of such a history. Is it worth the time, effort and expense to produce it? This resolves itself to two pertinent questions: What is the value of history? Does it make a valuable contribution to our present work and our outlook for the future? These questions are being raised to direct the mind of the reader to a much neglected emphasis. That is the value of history to the individual as a member of a community, church or society; and, of course, it logically follows as to whether we have given adequate consideration to the history of our work in the Congo. The author found the research work and the writing most interesting and inspiring, and very useful. We hope it shall be such for the reader. It is continually emphasized by statesmen that a knowledge of the history of a citizen's country and its leaders, makes for better and more intelligent citizenship. So it is hoped that the history of our work will stimulate greater interest and promote greater usefulness in the constituency. Our youth, as well as all of us, need to know the faith, the loyalty, the willing sacrifice and strenuous labor of those who labored at home and in the Congo, and into whose labors we have entered.

What, then, are some of the definite values to be received from the reading of history, especially a history of the church's work in the Congo?  In the first place, it helps us to more fully appreciate, understand, and evaluate the life, work, and atonement of Jesus Christ for the world. It is when we see the loyalty, faith and courage of our missionaries, as well as the marvelous transformation in the lives of the natives on the field, that we can understand better the great redemptive work of Christ for mankind. This faith of our fathers we must not forget, if we expect to go on in that same faith.  In the second place, history serves as a corrective for the work in which we are engaged. As a person studies the record of the work done, he does not only find successes and always efficiency; but the work also reveals failures, weaknesses, wrong judgments and inefficiency both from the standpoint of the missionaries and of the board. These experiences serve as a guide and corrective for our work now and in the future. The lamp of experience must always be kept burning brightly, if it is to give us proper light on the way. In the third place, history serves as a stabilizing influence in our mission work. Quite often as the board and the missionaries faced difficult and trying situations and problems, they were prone to think that they were new and were faced for the first time; and so, too, often, became unduly disturbed. But when we look to the past and study the records, we discover that these same problems and situations had arisen before, and that faithful men and women had to face them with faith and courage; and so we go on with larger vision, greater determination, and unflagging zeal.

Finally, history will only be valuable as it is read and used. It is accordingly hoped that it will be used in mission study classes and even furnish sermonic material. Since this book is naturally brief and the first one, it is hoped further by the writer that it may be used as source material for the further writing of history of various phases of our mission work in the Congo. The church should always attend to her historic continuity, preserve her rich heritage, and take definite measures to acquaint her membership with that heritage. It is the author's deep conviction that a church which isolates itself from its past and dedicates itself only to its present and future will eventually fail. It is only as we know, appreciate and use that heritage that it becomes of the largest value. May this effort then aid in bringing to us our great opportunity and responsibility in the great missionary enterprise. "To go into all the world and preach the gospel," was our Lord's last command before He ascended to the Father, indicating that this concern lay nearest to the Saviour's heart. It is said that the watchword of a Bantu Congregational Church is "Malihambe" which literally means, "Let it go." This does not mean "let it alone," or "forget it"; but it means "release the redemptive work of Christ for lost mankind." In this spirit may we go forth.

### GIVE A THOUGHT TO AFRICA

Give a thought to Africa!
'Neath the burning sun,
Hosts of weary hearts are there,
Waiting to be won.
Many idols have they,
But from swamp and clod
Many a voice is crying out
For the living God.

Breathe a prayer for Africa!
"O Thou God of love,

Send Thy blessings on the tribes
From Thy home above."
Swarthy lips when moved by grace
Can most sweetly sing;
Pray that Africa's heart may be
Loyal to our King.

Give your love to Africa!
There our brothers call.
Bring release from slavery,
Break sin's bitter thrall.
White shall love the black man,
Each forget the past;
In the Father's house above
All will meet at last.

# CHAPTER II

# Why Missions?

It is well in the beginning of a history of thirty-five years in the Congo to raise the question, "Why mission work in the Congo?" Or even the more general question, "Why missions?" Particularly in these days of crises and revolution which so seriously effect missions both at the home base as well as in the field, it becomes necessary to rethink, reexamine, reconsider and perhaps even rediscover the real purposes and motives for doing mission work, or continuing work in the countries beyond the sea.

The purposes and motives of an individual or group are always very essential in the efficiency and effectiveness of the work done. A motive gives vision, conviction, courage and effective service. It also has much to do with a person's loyalty to a cause. Some of the essentials in the consideration of motives are— first, whether we have well defined motives; second, whether the motives are selfish or unselfish; and third, what are the primary and secondary motives? It is possible to go to the Congo simply to bring the natives modern machinery, a western civilization, or even a denominational message. It is, of course, an established fact in the history of our thirty-five years in the Congo that our primary emphasis has been spiritual and not economic, educational or even medical. But on the other hand, we also learn that we could not ignore the economic, educational and medical in our program of work. It is rather a matter as to whether the spiritual or these others shall find first place and receive primary emphasis in our work. This difference in emphasis is well expressed in an answer given as to what missionaries are. Some one has said, "Missionaries are sent to preach, not experience, but redemption; not economics, but gospel; not culture, but conversion; not reforms, but liberation; not progress, but forgiveness; not social reform, but awakening; not a new organization, but a new creation; not civilization, but Christianity. We are ambassadors, not diplomats."

Further, in our consideration of missionary motives we must remind ourselves that sheer enthusiasm nor even consecration are not the only qualities essential in our great missionary task. In these days many programs and panaceas are offered and carried on with great consecration and enthusiasm, believing that they will be the solution for the world's sin and healing for the world's sorrow. These have been emphasized so much that it has dampened the enthusiasm of many church people for the only permanent solution—the gospel of Jesus Christ. The world cannot be redeemed by education, economic reforms, culture, civilization, or even disarmament; but the seeds of the kingdom of Christ must be planted in the hearts of men. The world is putting the church to shame by its enthusiasm and consecration to its worldly program. Commercialism and pleasure have made large sacrifices in spreading their message throughout the world. History records that missionaries and gold diggers often went together to open up new countries. It is historically true that in the three greatest outbursts of Christian activity outside that of the apostles, were at the same time military, exploring and commercial activities. So it behooves us, when Christian missions are at the cross roads, to reassure ourselves as to the fundamental purposes and motives of missions. Indifference to missions goes with indifference to Christianity.

There is a great deal of criticism of missions today and a great need for rethinking. We must discover anew the dynamic for missions. We can best defend missions by rediscovering the sense of a mission in the Christian life. There is an internal validity for missions. Missions has too often lost its passion and become merely a task. There is in Christianity a deeper insight, a more compelling passion, a vitalizing and transforming force which can not be found in any other religion in the world. This effects motives and purposes. The place to discover this transforming power is in the Word of God. The greatest book in the world is the Bible, and the proclamation of its central message is the world's most significant enterprise. The

"The Book of books for all people"

central theme of the Bible is a revelation of the divine provision for the needs of the world. It is redemption through Christ with a view of establishing the perfected kingdom of God.

What, then, is the primary motive of missions? The first answer is found in the nature and purpose of God — the revelation of the Eternal Redemptive Purpose of God for mankind. This revelation unfolds itself throughout the Bible both in the Old and New Testaments beginning with the call of Abraham in

the twelfth chapter of Genesis and running through to
the last chapter of the book of Revelation. Every book
of the Bible makes its definite contribution to this
theme of Redemption. So, if missionary zeal ever les-
sens, if the church loses its vision, or becomes indifferent to the command of our Lord; the first and un-
failing recourse must be to study anew with patience
and prayer, the oracles of God, the message of the
Prophets and Apostles, the inspired directory of service," which obligates the followers of Christ to speed
the gospel message to the uttermost parts of the earth.
This redemptive purpose of God always includes a
command and a promise. The external command, "Go
ye," and the promise, "I will go with you," are very
dependent upon this divine purpose. The lack of interest, and vision, and conviction in relation to missions
is usually due to a failure to see this purpose.

The great work of the missionary in the Congo
is not to make the native religious, nor to convince
him that there is a God, but rather to reveal to him
what God is like. This is fundamental today in our
world crisis. The philosophies of the world are all religious and set up gods of their own, but the serious-
ness of the situation is that these gods are not the Father of our Lord Jesus Christ. The motive, therefore,
of missions is not to increase the power and size of a
sect, or a desire for world conquest, or a conviction that
Christian principles promote prosperity; rather, its
real origin lies in the purpose, program, and command
of our heavenly Father. An individual is a missionary
whether at home or abroad, if he is a Christian. An
outward command to go becomes an inward imperative
and a great dynamic which grows out of the individual's relationship with God. The person is drawn into
missionary activity by a motive, rather than driven

by outside forces. It was Paul, the greatest missionary outside of Jesus, who said, "I am debtor," "I am an ambassador," "Woe is me, if I preach not the gospel," "The love of Christ constrains me," "For to me to live is Christ." Here we can see concretely the source of the motive for missions. It grows out of a deep and abiding experience with God through Christ.

What is this power which is the source of the primary motive of missions? It is the power of love — the love of God which produces rich fellowship in the church and a love for souls in the world. God is an active, seeking, loving, revealing God. The whole purpose of His Revelation is for Redemption. The complete and final Revelation of God for Redemption was through Jesus Christ. He came into the world to show us the Father; so that the love of God might save us and become a power in our lives. Paul refers to this gospel of love as the power of God unto salvation. This word, "power," has the same origin as the word, "dynamite" or "dynamo." Love was to be a force in the life of an individual or of a group. It is very important in these days that we decide in our own thinking whether the gospel of love is a power, a mere sentimentality, or even a weakness as the world today contends. We live in a world of power. This is revealed not only in Europe and Asia, but in our country as well. The history of civilization is the history of various kinds of power. We find today great political, material, and military power. The sad thing is that much of this power is used for destruction, rather than for constructive and creative purposes. The fault lies not in the power, but in the use that is made of it. A knife in the hands of a physician may save a life, while in the hands of a criminal it means destruction. It all depends on the motives and purposes of men.

Jesus came into a world of force. The Roman Empire was built on material and military power. The Greeks emphasized intellectual power. Jesus came into such a world and revealed by His life, teachings, death and resurrection the power of love. There was an irresistible conflict between the power of the world and the power of love, good will, and peace of Jesus. Jesus was tempted by Satan in the wilderness to use the world's power to accomplish His purposes, but He resisted the temptation and lived the life of love. Jesus said to His disciples, "A new commandment I give you," meaning that love should be the ruling power in their lives. Our Heavenly Father created the universe in this love. We live in a friendly universe created by our living, loving Father. He also created man in love when He made him in His own image. This is the reason for our freedom and power of choice. All of Jesus' life, teaching, and ministry of healing bear witness of this power of love. He went about doing good.

But the greatest revelation and manifestation of this power of love came on Calvary. Jesus, through love, shed His blood for the remission of sins. The outpouring love of Christ on the cross reveals the Father's love in its longest reach. This manifestation of love was new. It was a dying love. Jesus said this dying love is a sign of discipleship. It was Tertullian who one hundred and fifty years later said about the early Christians, "See how these Christians love each other and how ready they are to die for each other." This power of love in the heart of a redeemed person is why we have missions. This missionary spirit will pervade every life that is redeemed whether its expression is given in the Congo or at home. This is the message that the Christian lives, and preaches, and teaches to the uttermost parts of the earth.

This eternal redemptive purpose of God reached then its highest reality in the Incarnation of Jesus. This is why the message of Jesus is good news because it reveals the Father so full of grace and truth. Through Him man finds redemption and co-operates with Him in the great work of the Kingdom. This redemptive experience with the Father is the rootage of life out of which comes the fruitage of efficient Christian living and service. In-so-far as we partake of the Divine Nature of our Heavenly Father, we shall want to follow Jesus in His far reaching purpose to save lost souls with a complete salvation. There is only one salvation and that is through Christ. The missionary who goes to the Congo, goes with this Christ experience. It determines his life, his enthusiasm, passion for souls and his witness. He is there to proclaim his love of God to the natives. This gives both motivation to his conduct and power for the accomplishment of his God-given task. The wealth of our Christian missions does not lie in our buildings or equipment, but in the power and personality of our missionaries. Every interest and every relationship must be brought under the domination of Christ's mind and spirit. He must become Saviour and Lord.

But all of these challenges simply emphasize that the church must have adequate power to meet the needs of the world. There can be no withdrawals, retrenchments, or timid compromises in this great missionary program. The supreme need of the hour is greater spiritual power. This can only come through fellowship with Christ. Numbers, organization, equipment and wealth cannot be substituted for this transforming power through Christ. It is very true, what Phllips Brooks said, "In this world of shallow believers and weary workers how we need the Holy Spirit.

He can, however, help us the most when we open our hearts and ask Him to come in." Thus we need consecrated personality, creative thinking and efficient service.

The church of Jesus Christ, then, is by nature a missionary church. The church in its missionary efforts is often tempted to place too much emphasis on its own ideas, programs and organizations, rather than upon the central idea which is fellowship with Christ. He who was the beating heart of the New Testament must be the pulsating center of the church of today. It is the living church of the living God. In the second place, the church then becomes a fellowship of the saved. The holiness of the church is incomplete but not unreal. In the third place, such a church is missionary in

¹⁄₁₀ FOR THE LORD

⁹⁄₁₀ FOR YOUR SELF

## DO YOU GIVE YOUR SHARE?

its spirit and service. Finally, the church becomes universal and united, not because of outward pressure but because of its inward spirit. This is what our Lord had in mind when He gave the great commission as recorded in Matt. 28. The gospel is good news which is to be published abroad. Individuals are to become adventurers as they go forth to herald this Good News; for the gospel of Jesus Christ not only has a universal message but brings a world salvation. A shrinking and desperate world is in need of this expanding gospel. The church dare not bring anything less than kindled hearts and enlarged vision to that need.

> I know of lands that are sunk in shame,
> Of hearts that faint and tire;
> But I know of a Name, a Name, a Name
> That can set those lands on fire.
> Its sound is a brand, its letters flame,
> I know a Name, a Name, a Name
> That will set those lands on fire!

In this great missionary enterprise we inherit the inspiration of mighty spirits who have dreamed, desired, dared, endured, suffered, sacrificed and won great achievements. We do not need a new gospel, but we need to know how the old gospel can be restated so it will reveal applications to the present day.

The final answer, then, as to why we engage in mission work is that Christianity is a missionary message that God is the Father of life, and Jesus Christ the Saviour of men. The imperative for missions is not an argument but a passion. No one argued with David Livingstone to go to the Congo. His sense of need and a constraining passion of love sent him. This conviction was born of knowledge, experience and inward compulsion. When we lose this passion and imperative we must come back to the cross to find it. The redeemed person shared in God's redemptive work. The poet has beautifully expressed it thus:

> Me seems it renders God great joy to see,
> Hands stirring after His creatively,
> Yea, that He even left a part undone
> That we might finish that by Him begun,
> And help Him with our efforts to erect
> His house, as masons help an architect.

With such a spirit not only will the church be missionary in its message and program, but each member will feel his or her responsibility to support this work of the Kingdom. We support missions because there is in our hearts a sense of a mission. We become indifferent to missions as we become indifferent to our own Christian life and experience. Missions must remain the fruitage of a conviction and passion, and not become a mere work to be done. There is sin, and the wages of sin is death. Man has need of salvation and only Christ is sufficient. So the missionary, God filled, God directed and God empowered, goes to lift up Christ in His life, death and resurrection.

Finally, we believe in missions because: (1) We must recognize that the desperate situation in the world today can not be remedied by reformation, but only by redemption and regeneration. (2) Definite decision must be made to accept redemption in Christ producing a new character and not merely improvement along the old ways of life. (3) To accept Christ means to adopt His teachings as the practical plan of life in social, industrial, and international relationships, as well as in personal conduct. (4) A definite Biblical foundation is needed in thought and preaching. (5) Evangelism must be carried to the people wherever they are and applied to their needs. (6) This is the work of the laity as well as the ministry. (7) Evangelism must be world-wide, not merely local. Matt. 28:19-20 is the charter of the Christian missionary enterprise. Also John 3:14-17. Jesus announces the aim, field and obligation of the church. He is supreme in authority, understanding and power. In Christ there is abundant life. The pressure of our present world situation demands that we make a fresh effort to understand all Jesus meant by His teaching about the Kingdom. It is

almost unbelievable that men confessing to be redeemed and regenerated are still debating about the obli-
gations of Christian stewardship. They are trifling with
God and their souls.

> Set us afire, Lord;
> Stir us we pray;
> While the world perishes
> We go our way,
> Purposeless, passionless,
> Day after day.
> Set us afire, Lord;
> Stir us we pray.

## CHAPTER III

# The Land of the Open Door

Africa has often been called the dark continent, land of the jungles, the land of mystery. But with the tremendous changes that have been and are taking place, it can just as truthfully be called "the emerging continent, the land of great opportunity, the Africa that is 'coming to be,' or the land of the open door." For this continent, which one hundred years ago was practically unknown except the northern part and a few trading posts along the coast, is now open to the nations of the world and nine-tenths of it has been partitioned to the European nations. It is a land of unmeasured natural resources and inestimable human treasures.

Africa, the second largest continent in the world, is five thousand miles long from north to south and forty-five hundred miles wide from east to west. Its northern end lies in the same latitude as Washington, D. C., while its southern end is in the latitude of Buenos Aires. Its land area comprises nearly one-fourth of the globe, its area being 11,800,000 square miles. It is twice the size of all Europe, or three times the size of the United States. You could place on this continent, United States, British Isles, Germany, France, Norway and Sweden, Italy, Argentina, China, India and Spain, and then have enough room left for several Belgiums. Its coast line is equal to the distance around the world. There are four outstanding divisions of this continent: Northern Africa, north of the Sahara Desert; the Sahara Desert; the territory south of the Sahara, which is the Congo basin; and the southern end of Africa.

The contour of the continent can perhaps best be described by saying that it has a narrow sea coast all around it a few hundred miles wide. Next to the sea coast are found mountains and hills almost all the way around Africa. Inside of these mountains are found the plateau regions. Africa has four large rivers which drain the continent. Three of the four rivers find their source in the territory of the lakes in the east central part of Africa. The Nile flows north, the Congo west and south, and the Zambezi south. The Niger River is located in the western part of Africa, south of the Sahara Desert and flows into the Gulf of Guinea. It is these large rivers that help to make the interior of Africa accessible to the explorers, traders and missionaries. Africa has forty thousand miles of navigable rivers. It is in these large river basins where we find the natives and where civilization began.

The equator runs midway of the continent, so that most of Africa is located in the Torrid Zone. This means that in most of Africa there are only two seasons, the rainy and the dry. The unfavorable climate of most of Africa was one of the great obstacles to exploration and missionary work.

Africa has a population of 142,000,000 people. Of these only about 12,000,000 are free citizens. The rest are natives of the colonies of the European countries. North of the equator are found the Hamites mixed with Semitic people and also negroes. In the southern end of Africa are found the Bushmen and Hottentots. The largest group, found in most of Africa, are the dark brown people or negroids, called the Bantus. Every ninth person in the world lives in Africa. The colored race of Africa doubles once in every forty years while the white race doubles only once in eighty years. Over nine-tenth of the Africans are reached today by

European and American commerce, but only a little over one-tenth have been reached by the gospel.

The continent of Africa has great and abundant resources. Some of these are ivory, rubber, gold, copper, tin, oils, radium, copal gum, cobalt, diamonds and agricultural products. Most of these resources are produced by the native. These were the resources which commercial companies exploited. Later, the nations discovered that the soil was one of the outstanding resources of Africa. The greatest resource, however, is not its mines, forests and soil, but the natives themselves. The earliest civilization in all of Africa is that in the Nile valley. This civilization is not only the oldest in Africa, but one of the oldest in the world. The history of Egypt is very prominent in the history of the Old and New Testaments.

Our chief interest in the history of our mission work lies in that part of Africa which is the very heart of it, the Belgian Congo. This territory was the last to be discovered and explored, because it is in the interior of Africa and its climate was not conducive either to trade or the work of missions. The Congo territory has nearly 10,000,000 square miles and about 11,000,000 population. It is drained by the Congo River which rises in the lake regions of the east and runs north and west until the mountains deflect it south and west to the sea. Over 1,000,000 cubic feet of water per second are poured by it into the Atlantic Ocean. The pulse of the river can be felt fifty miles out and its waters color the ocean for over a hundred miles. The Congo River and its large tributaries are navigable for six thousand miles. Twenty thousand miles of forest are found along its banks. There are four thousand islands in the river, several of them ten miles long. It has many sand banks which make hazardous traveling in

boats and small steamers. The Congo River has nearly a thousand miles navigable water without cataracts
between Leopoldville and Stanleyville. The Kasai
River is one of its largest tributaries. It is along this
river where the southern Presbyterian mission of Luebo is situated and our own Charlesville station.

This territory of the Congo, because of the climate,
forests and hostile natives, was not explored nor missionary work established until the nineteenth century.
It is largely because of this fact that this part of Africa
particularly has been referred to as pagan or dark
Africa. The Congo was dark from the standpoint of
exploration or civilization, but particularly because it
did not have the light of the gospel. It is, as Dr. Emory
Ross states, "Although we call Africa the dark continent, it today, positively glistens. It glistens with
diamonds, nearly the whole world's supply of them.
Glistens with gold, mountains of copper and much of
the globe's radium, and soon it will glisten with elec-
tricity since it has nearly a fourth of the world's water
power.  But what we are most interested in, Africa
glistens with the uplifted eyes of a hundred and forty
million of the earth's people. They are waiting for the
gospel of Jesus Christ. Africa awaits us. The door is
open. As one of our great missionaries has said. 'The
pioneering work is largely done and dangers and hardships diminished. The Bantu races covering millions
of square miles are now accessible to the gospel. They
have been introduced to the knowledge of the civilized
world. May they be speedily embraced in the love of
the Christian church.' "

The question may be raised by the reader as to
why this discussion on physical features and contour of
the land of Africa and the Congo, when we are interested in our mission work there. The reason lies in

the fact that the natural environment of any people is a great determining factor in their way of living and their civilization. People of the city are different from rural people because of their environment. In like manner people in Temperate Zones are different from those in the Torrid Zone, and people living in the mountains different from those in the valleys. Therefore, we must take account of the environment of the Congo because of its effect on the people who live there. The heat, high atmospheric humidity, dry and wet seasons, the forest lands and the open spaces all help to determine the life of the natives and directly effect mission work there. The constituency at home, the mission board and candidates for the mission field should study seriously these geographical factors that mean so much in the life of a people. Perhaps one illustration will suffice. When factories were established at Leopoldville and natives were taken from their villages and natural surroundings and were introduced to industrial life and city environment, it created a great problem physically, intellectually and morally. The outward environment effected the mind and heart of the native. The movement today in the Congo of preserving the tribal life of the natives and the surroundings in which they were wont to live is proof of the fact just stated.

One of the most interesting chapters in the history of Africa is that of how civilization came to its various parts. As stated before, the earliest civilization was found along the northern coast of Africa in the country called Egypt. In the days of Jesus and Paul the Roman Empire included north Africa in its boundaries. In fact, the name Africa comes from the wrod, "Afriga," which was the name of a Berber community, a Roman province in northern Africa.

The first explorers, however, to come to the west coast of southern and central Africa were the Portuguese. This was the beginning of the age of reawakening of the nations. This Renaissance led to discovery and exploration. The first outstanding explorer, who later became king of Portugal, was Prince Henry. He became interested as early as 1415 A. D. after his defeat of the Mohammedan power. From this time until 1500 the Portuguese went down the west coast and rounded the southern end of Africa. Their direct purpose was not to explore, but rather to seek a route to India and the East Indies. In 1407 Bartholomew Diaz discovered the mouth of the Congo and by 1497 had gone as far south as the Cape of Good Hope. In 1507 Vasco Da Gama went around the southern end of Africa and explored along the east coast as far north as Mombasa. It can rightly be said that Prince Henry and Vasco Da Gama of Portugal put Africa on the map. The Portuguese were not interested in exploring the interior, but rather wanted trade posts along the coast for commercial reasons. It was Portugal that began the slave trade (called "black ivory") which became such an evil in the nineteenth century. She would send native slave traders to the interior to bring them to the coast, then take the slaves to Brazil and India to work on her plantations.

The hold of the Portuguese on Africa, however, was short lived because of a changed situation in Europe. Through war and conquest Portugal was annexed to Spain in 1580. Spain's rule was brief when her sea power was destroyed in the defeat of the Spanish Armada in 1588 by the English. This gave the Dutch their opportunity to seize the colonial empire of the Portuguese, and they continued in the slave trade and the establishing of trading posts. In the beginning of the seventeenth century the English and French became inter-

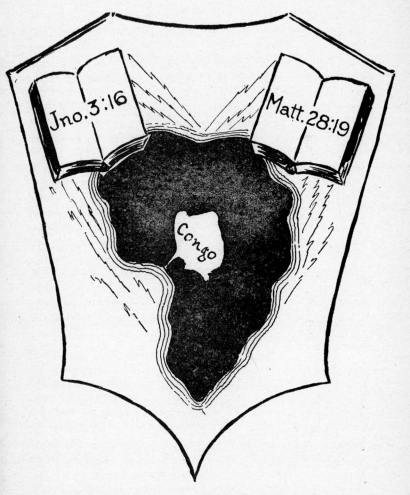

"The Congo, a part of our accepted responsibility"

ested in exploration and the building of colonial em-
pires. Practically all the European countries were now

seeking routes to the East Indies and India in order to establish trade. In fact, it may truthfully be said that by the lure of India and the spice islands of the Orient both America and Africa were discovered and explored because they came in the path of this search for trade routes to the East.

The beginning of the establishment of colonies in southern Africa came in the first part of the seventeenth century. The English and the Dutch began to establish themselves there. The first definite action was taken for settlement by England through the organization called the African Association of London which later became the Royal Geographical Society. Up to this time the nations' interest in Africa was largely the slave trade. These slaves seemed necessary in their colonial possessions, even in Virginia of the thirteen colonies. It was only when England, France and Germany became industrial powers and were in great need of raw materials and food stuffs, that they became interested in the interior of Africa. By 1850 a number of the nations had established spheres of influence and special privilege in Africa.

Of all the territories open to civilization, the one of greatest interest was the opening of the Belgian Congo. Up to 1850 very little was known as to the interior of this vast territory. There lay the very storehouse of the nations of the world, untouched and unused.

There are two men to whom must be given the largest credit for the opening up of the Congo to civilization. These were David Livingstone and Henry M. Stanley. It is the purpose in this chapter to discuss Livingstone as an explorer. He came to the southern part of Africa as a missionary but spent a great deal of time in discovery and exploration. He followed the Zambezi River to its source and made most of his ex-

plorations in the territory of the great lakes region of
eastern Africa. The question which was asked since the
days of Nero, the emporer, "Where is the source of the
Nile?" was also an unanswered question to David Livingstone. It was left to Henry M. Stanley, who was sent
to Africa by James Gordon Bennett, the editor of the
New York Herald to find Livingstone. He found him
by the east shore of Lake Tanganyika at Ujiji, then
returned to England for help and supplies and to report to the Royal Geographical Society. It was in his
second trip that Stanley followed the Congo River
north to what is now Stanleyville and on to the very
mouth of the river traveling over fifteen hundred miles
and all of that through territory where no white man
had ever traveled.

It was as a result of the explorations of Livingstone and Stanley that Leopold II, king of Belgium,
(1865-1909) became interested in this territory and in
1876 formed an International Association of Africa
with himself at the head to explore the Congo and discover its resources. The other nations gave their consent to such an organization. This association had several outstanding purposes. One was to open the interior
to commerce, industry, and to scientific enterprise.
Another was to consider measures for abolishing the
terrible scourge of slavery known to prevail over wide
and populous territories in the interior of Africa. The
seat of this African Association was to be at Brussels.
It was international in the sense that any nation could
collect funds and co-operate in the project. Leopold of
Belgium was the most active and became the organizer
and builder of the Congo Free State. It was through
the influence of Leopold that Stanley was sent on his
second journey and while in the Congo established
many stations and made four hundred treaties with

various native chiefs. In 1885 a congress was held in Berlin, Germany to adjust the claims of various nations in relation to the Congo. Representatives from United States attended this meeting. They decided that slavery must cease and allowed Leopold II to continue his personal leadership in the Congo. From this time on the Congo became a grab bag for the nations of Europe. Concessions were granted by Leopold II to various companies for the development of resources in the Congo. This territory remained under the leadership of Leopold II until 1908 when the Congo Free State became the Belgian Congo and was placed under the supervision of the Belgium government. This action was taken for reasons which will be discussed in a later chapter.

With this brief history we see that Africa is passing out of its isolation into daily contacts with western civilization. As soon as the black man meets the white man, the black man's education has begun and this education is moulding the African of the future. Commerce has been one of the great teachers and Africa's greatest pioneering power. Nine-tenth of the continent is now affected by white civilization. The supreme task now is to guard and guide these new forces, so they may bless and not curse the people, because the final goal for the African is, after all, that he may find abundant life through Jesus Christ. The fog of mystery and dread which hung over the continent south of the Sahara for countless ages was penetrated seventy-five years ago by shafts of light. When Dr. Stanley made his report to Europe of what he had found, they did not believe it. But today this territory is covered with railroads, highways, telephone and telegraph lines.

Where seventy-five years ago the African hunted his game, today are cultivated fields producing good crops; and where its trade was reckoned at $150,000,000, it is now reckoned at $3,000,000,000. In spite of the many interesting features, geographical and zoological, the most interesting is that of man. This native that has been exploited and used as a commodity in a time of slavery, must have his life developed; so that he may be able to develop the resources of his own territory.

CHAPTER IV

# Religion In Native Life

There are three qualifications for a skilled workman in any calling, but especially is this true in the
work of a missionary. First, he must have a knowledge of the tools he is going to use, which to the missionary would be his general knowledge, but particularly his knowledge of the Bible. This was emphasized in our second chapter. The second is that he knows
how to use the tools effectively. This, for the missionary, means how to get the message of the Bible
to the natives. The third is a knowledge of the material
on which the tools are to be used. This is particularly
vital from the standpoint of our missionary work. The
missionary must know the native. He should make
a deep and sympathetic study of every phase of native
life. He should understand the native's physical life
and his attempts in providing himself with economic
goods. It is important to know the kind of mentality
the native has. Finally, the missionary should know
the native's relationships with each other and the place
of his religion in all these different interests of life.
The mind of the native is not like a white piece of paper with nothing written on it, nor like a blackboard
where you can erase what is there. The native has
ideas, feelings and a will. These powers in his life
must be understood; so that he may be guided aright
to the Christ who can transform his life. No African
native needs to become an American before Christ
can dwell in his heart. Missionaries must meet the
native where he is, if they wish to lead him where he
ought to be.

Of all the resources and assets that are to be found in Africa the greatest is the native. Since our interest in this history lies particularly in the Congo Inland Mission's territory, we shall limit ourselves to the natives as we find them in the Congo. They are called the Bantu people. There are five to twenty-five persons to the square mile in the Congo. The Bantu people are found from five degrees north of the Equator to the south coast. "Bantu" or Aba-ntu is the plural of a word which means human being. There are 40,-000,000 Bantus covering one-third of the continent. As said before, they are not negroes but are negroid, a people of brownish color. These natives have many languages and dialects, most of which are not yet written. The social and cultural traits of the Bantu people are very similar but their languages are very different. There are over two hundred dialects in the Congo alone.

These natives, particularly in the territory of our mission field, live in villages usually ranging in size of from one hundred to five hundred people. The villages are usually from five to twenty-five miles apart. The thing to know above everything else in the Congo is the native village, since each village is an African world,—particularly is this true of the Bantu people. It is so because of the relation of the native to his village and the submerging of the individual to the interests of the group. Although with the tremendous changes that have come about through modern civilization and the removing of natives from their villages to industrial cities, the native still thinks in terms of his village and his tribe. In fact, as stated before, since about 1930 steps are being taken to revive the original habitat of the native. The form of government of the village in its primitive state and at the time our

mission work began, is tribal with a chief at the head
and with sub-chiefs and a council of elders. Either the
family, clan, or tribe account for everything in the native's life. He as an individual counts for very little.
The loyalty of the native to his chief, to the medicine
man, and even to his dead ancestors must be explained
in the light of his communal life. The women of the village live in a plane far below that of the men. They
are chattels held as just so much property. Polygamy
is universal. The chief's wealth is determined by the
number of wives that he has. The men of the village
hunt and fish, while the women do the hard work and
provide the rest of the food outside of the meat. The
woman is only important as the mother of children
through whom blood relationships must be determined.
She lives, not for herself, but for the tribe.

Although these natives of the Congo have lived
lives of ignorance, superstition and fear, which has
often produced in them evil conduct; yet they have
good qualities in their lives as well as bad. By their
deepest nature they are law abiding, inoffensive and
friendly, except as they are stirred to anger by brutal
officials, fear of war, or injustice. Evidence of this is
shown in the fact that very few soldiers are needed in
the Congo to control the territory. These people are
simple, child like, lovable, very loyal in their friend-
ships but ruled continually by the great power of fear.
The condition of the native, with his own life of fear
and the sudden added impact of our modern civilization is well expressed by Rev. John M. Springer in
the Congo Mission News for January, 1932. "Rawest
heathen villages felt the sudden impact of full-orbed,
aggressive modern civilization almost over night. The
few crude tools which had been used for countless
centuries were displaced in the hands of many by the

"Visible results of outstation school work"

latest inventions of a mechanical age.

The effect on the native people at first was fairly stupefying. The total revolution in almost every phase of native life has been stupendous. Not a tribe of villages within hundreds of miles of these great mining centers, but has been called upon for all available man power. Bewilderment—confusion—necessity of learning new tasks under unaccustomed conditions, exposure to legions of seductive temptations, rapid increase of income with teeming supplies of articles on which to spend it, idleness for the women and the inevitable consequences, are but a few of the features of the new life. Confusing has been the experience of these passing years." The same condition is described by Dr. Emory Ross when he says, "In the years since 1877 everything that we know with accuracy about the Congo has transpired. And one of the things we know

"Outstation teacher and pupils in the Congo"

is this: never before in the history of the world has so primitive a people in so large an area had the full weight of so advanced a civilization put upon them in so short a time. The whole impact has come within a single lifetime. And in the Congo we have the amazing, the unique spectacle of the very sons and grandsons of the men who repeatedly ambushed Stanley and more than once carried off the dripping flesh of his followers to their waiting villages, shouting 'Nyama! Nyama!' (Meat! meat!)—the sons and grandsons of these aged cannibals, some of whom still live, aiding in one of the swiftest and most lucrative of economic penetrations the world has ever seen."

As the missionary becomes acquainted with Bantu native, he discovers that God has not left himself without a witness even in the Congo. The native has a religion very sacred to him and his faith is woven into the full pattern of his life. There is, however, much of his religious life which is immoral and even antagonistic to the teaching of the gospel. There are many things in their customs, folk lore, sayings, attitudes and actions which serve as signs to the missionary as to the need of the native religiously. The customs of the native should be studied carefully for they are the cornerstone of his morality. The Bantu native has a great natural capacity for religion.

The African has two great articles of faith,—belief in a creator God and belief in the survival of the dead and human personality. Out of these articles of faith there are two principles which emerge. The first is that of kinship which is the element that holds the tribe together. The second is their ritual worship, the worship of spirits. This religion is called animism.

The political conception of the native as to his relation to the tribe and to his family is not only political, but also religious. The family is the unit of society and relationship is determined through the mother. If any individual in the family dies, he is not lost to the group, but simply initiated into the unseen family of the departed dead. The native believes that the dead live in the underworld in families, villages, and tribes, as they did while living in this world. These departed people really live in the lives of the natives. They worship their dead, not because of love, but because of fear of these spirits that have departed. The natives have their sacred places where these spirits are supposed to be, and so their ancestor worship is an essential part of the faith by which they live. The spirit of their ancestors is there either to bless their lives and protect them, or to curse them and bring evil upon them.

It is the second principle, however, which holds the largest place in the life of the native, his worship of the spirits. They conceive of everything about them, — every tree, every hill, every rock or spring, — as having a soul or spirit. These spirits dominate his thought continually. He lives in a haunted land. Just as we think of germs being everywhere in the air, so the native thinks of his surroundings as being infested with spirits. Most of these spirits are malicious and want to injure someone; so he tries to appease them through sacrifices. His religion of fear weighs on his soul like lead. He is fetish ridden, tortured in mind and body; and when he is the most religious, he becomes the most fiendish. All important events in the life of the native from birth to death are marked by religious ceremonies. The birth of a child, the naming of it, the transition from childhood into youth, marriage, important decisions as adults, and death are all marked by religious rites. He lives as a superstitious man walking in a dark forest, **always** afraid someone may jump out from behind a tree to hurt him, or like a man walking along a dark road who feels as if a sheeted ghost may start out from some bush at any moment and he may be caught in its clammy hands.

The reason the native lives such a life of fear and panic, is because he lives in a universe where there is no God of love, nor moral order and no security. There is only accident and confusion. In his life things can happen without cause. He thinks nature is cruel to him. He worships because he is afraid. He has a child mind; hence is superstitious and imaginative. He makes no distinction between the natural and the supernatural. He can not distinguish between truth and error. He believes in a God who created things, but he thinks of him as a great African chief, rich and powerful, who has contempt for the native. He is afraid of his god. The danger of this modern civilization is that if you lift him out of this kind of a faith by modern industrial life and mechanical skill, you change only his outward situation and leave him a wanderer on a stormy sea. He needs first of all the power of the redemptive Christ. He needs to be taught to pray to a Heavenly Father as he now, being a heathen, pleads the spirits for help.

Where does this native turn for help when he is continually surrounded by terrifying spirits that can live either in animate or inanimate objects? He is willing to purchase safety by the most dreadful rites and sacrifices. Here is where the medicine man comes in. According to the native he knows the spirit world. The native must ally himself with the good spirits with the help of the medicine man, and try to protect himself from the evil spirits or witches which may be found in the brook, in his path, or in the tree tops. A person in the village may become a witch and bring a curse to the whole village. The medicine man can ferret out these witches, appease them and drive them away; so, regardless of how terrible the medicine man's commands may be, they have to be obeyed.

One illustration may help us to realize the place which the medicine man holds in the life of the native. Several women of a village had heard the roar of a

A native medicine man

lion near by and three young men went to kill the lion, one of whom was the son of the chief. In the struggle with the lion the chief's son was hurt very badly. His arm and sides were torn by the lion's claws. The boys, however, killed the lion; but when the wounded boy came back to the  village, the natives called on the witch doctor to help the boy. He put on his costume of grass with his hideous mask and horns.  He stood there an ugly and grotesque figure. He made the people gather in a circle with the wisest men of the village. He mixed some roots and herbs with clay and plastered them on the open wounds of the boy muttering as he worked. He was calling on the spirits to aid him in finding out who was responsible for this calamity. The people had entirely forgotten the other two brave boys who killed the lion, or the fact that the lion was dead. The question with the witch doctor was, "Had the people neglected an offering to their gods or the performing of rites due to their ancestral spirit? Were the spirits angry? Or did some enemy send the lion?" Soon there was weird dancing of the witch doctor in the fire light as he shook the (diviner basket) and called on the spirits. Finally the signs in the basket pointed to a shaky old woman as the guilty one. The natives, in anger, got rid of the woman who was supposed to be the guilty one. The wounded boy's arm was swelling larger and larger. Finally the chief, who knew of the missionaries, said to the witch doctor, "I'll take my boy to the white doctor at the mission." The boy was cared for and returned with his father to the village. The result of all this was that the village got rid of their witch doctor, the three young men who killed the lion went to the mission school, and became fine Christian workers. This illustrates the contrast between the superstitious life of fear and the work of the witch doctor on the one hand, and Christian faith and service on the other.

The witch doctor mentioned above represents another factor in the religion of animism,—that the spirit dwells in objects. These objects are called fetishes. This fetish may be a shell, a small horn, or any trinket that has been charged with spirit power. It becomes a fetish when the medicine man has consecrated it as such. Sacrifice offerings are made to these images and fetishes. These sacrifices may be animals of different kinds, a sheep, goat or chicken. The shedding of blood is very important in these sacrifice offerings. In primitive times people were even offered as sacrifices. The sacrifice offerings are often used to bring rain, cleanse the village of pestilence. The charms or fetishes are used to bring good luck or to keep away the evil spirits. So the medicine man becomes the native's protector, guide, adviser and interpreter. He is faith healer, priest, fortune teller, detective, magician, and occasionally even political boss. He sometimes has power greater than even the chief of the village.

The religion of the native is not only for this life, but also for the future. To the Bantu, to live after death is not a matter of argument but an axiom of life. The very way that they bury their dead is an evidence of their belief in a future life. To the Bantu, the soul and the body are separate. They even believe that while they are sleeping their souls walk and talk with the dead.

All this discussion has been given, because the writer believes that the Christian missionary can most effectively bring the gospel of Jesus Christ to these natives as he understands the life and religion of the native. Their deeply religious life, after all, reveals the fact that they are made in the image of God. It is this religious spirit which gives the missionary an opportunity and presents to him a challenge to bring Christ to the heart and life of the pagan native. The missionary should study their rituals to see whether it sheds some light on the discovery of the Bantu soul, as he studies their language and dialect so he might interpret their ideas. But as the native wanders in this maze of error and fear and in the dark shadow of animism, he needs the full light of Jesus Christ. He must be set free by the gospel from his bondage of fear. He must be taught that he lives in a universe controlled by the will of the Heavenly Father, and that there is a way of life which has meaning, and purpose, and power. The missionary needs to emphasize Jesus' teachings, the parables, and Paul's emphasis on the new birth and the new life.

The Belgian Congo has many problems in relation to agriculture, industry and government; but its greatest is the human problem, the native. He needs the message of the gospel of love and faith to dispel hate and fear. He is in great need of a friend. He looks upon the missionary as a friend, teacher, healer and guide. He needs the missionary because, if the missionary is true, he is the incarnation of the greatest friend and brother, Jesus Christ. The native may have difficulty in understanding our historical Christianity or some of the doctrines of the church; but he can be assured that when he is saved he is no more in the power of nature, or ancestral spirits, or fetishes, but has as his guide a light that shines amid the darkness of his fears. It must, however, always be kept in mind by both the missionary and the mission board, that a convert from the native life of animism can not at one moment eliminate all of what hundreds of generations have woven into every strand of his nature. The tares will still come up in the wheat field even after he has been converted.

### CHAPTER V

# Opening the Interior for Missions

David Livingstone said, "The end of exploration is the beginning of missionary enterprise." Africa, in the nineteenth century was the great field for discovery and exploration, as America had been in the fifteenth and sixteenth. The appropriation of Africa by the nations was very slow in the heart of Africa from 1800 to 1875. Missionary work was extremely difficult in this same period. Appropriation and missions waited upon exploration. Beginning about 1850 the darkness of the continent began to disappear. Men penetrated farther and farther inland. This opening of the interior is a story of adventure, courage, sacrifice and determination. One of the interesting facts of history is that when a new territory is opened for exploration and commercial purposes the missionary accompanies the explorer with the gospel of Jesus Christ. Quite often the explorer is also a missionary.

Both of these facts are true in the opening of Africa as well as the Congo. In fact, Prince Henry of Portugal, although an explorer was also animated by a desire to promote Christian faith and to stem the tide of Mohammedanism in the fifteenth century. By 1491 Dominican missionaries from Portugal had established mission stations along the west coast by the mouth of the Congo River. The Jesuits came in the sixteenth century from Italy to strengthen the mission work of the Portuguese already established. These early attempts, however, were almost fruitless because of the climatic conditions, the geographical barriers, and the hostility of the natives. This period of early mis-

sionary work was from 1491 to 1717. An explorer of the
Congo in 1816 said he could find no traces of this early
mission work except a few crucifixes and relics.

Real effective missionary work began at the close
of the eighteenth and the beginning of the nineteenth
centuries. The Moravians, as usual, were among the
earliest in the beginning of the eighteenth century. It is
said that Dr. Robert Moffat, on his first furlough to
England from his south African mission told Livingstone of "a vast plain to the north where he had sometimes seen in the morning sun the smoke of a thousand
villages where no missionary had ever been." The condition is also well described by Dr. Robert Laws, a
missionary to the territory around Lake Nyasa who
said, in 1875, "I could start from these hills, speaking
of a hill fifteen hundred feet high behind the pioneer
station at Cape Maclear, Lake Nyasa, and walk westward, westward, week after week, meeting thousands
of villages, millions of people, and until I came to the
west coast of Africa I would not meet with a single
missionary nor find one when I arrived there. Think of
all that vast region with its millions of inhabitants and
no one seeming to care for their souls."

The mission work in Africa by the Protestants began about 1800 A. D. The Baptists of England organized a missionary society October 2, 1792 to carry the
gospel to unevangelized territories. The inspiration for
this organization came from a sermon by William Car-
ey, a missionary to India who made the memorable
statement, "Expect great things from God, attempt
great things for God." The London Missionary Society was organized October 4, 1794 for the evangelization of territories where Christ is unknown. This society sent out such men as Robert Moffat, David Livingstone, and John Mackenzie, the father of the late

President Mackenzie of Hartford Theological Seminary. So by the time of David Livingstone the churches in Europe had only touched the fringe of the coast of Africa at several places. The most effective work thus far had been done by Dr. Robert Moffat who came to Cape Town in 1817.

The most effective work done in the opening of the interior of Africa for missions was the explorations of Livingstone and Stanley. David Livingstone was born in Blantyre, Scotland, March 19, 1813. He went to the University of Glasgow and received his diploma in medicine in 1840. He was ordained the same year. He had decided to go to China as a missionary but because of the Opium War the way was closed. While he was waiting in London he happened to attend a meeting where he heard Dr. Moffat speak on the needs of Africa. Livingstone, after speaking personally with Dr. Moffat, decided to go as a missionary. He sailed in August, 1840 for Cape Town. He took with him five hundred copies of Dr. Moffat's translation of the New Testament. He stayed at Cape Town until 1843 when he went to Kuruman, a mission station north of Cape Town. Here he was married in 1844 to Mary, the oldest daughter of Dr. Moffat. During the time 1843 to 1852 Livingstone was not only interested in missionary work, but sought to make exploring expeditions into the interior of Africa. Because of his deep interest in explorations, he felt that he was not able to keep up a home life, so he sent his family to Scotland, April 23, 1852. He literally fulfilled the words of the Master, "He that follows me must forsake wife and children, houses and lands." This home that was thus broken up, was the only one he had in Africa.

On November 11, 1853 he struck out from the upper waters of the Zambezi and traveled for six and a half months until he arrived at Loanda, on the west coast May 31, 1854. He crossed Africa from east to west in a higher latitude than anyone before him. He opened up a new country to Europe. When he came to Loanda he was very weak and rested several months in the home of the British consul. While here he had an opportunity to go home to England, but he refused because he felt he should go back east with his black companions. He returned to the Zambezi region in September, 1855. He then struck out eastward from this region and arrived at the coast May 21, 1856. He now went home to see his family, and spent two years in England and Scotland. He returned to Africa in 1858, taking his wife with him from 1858 to 1863. He made great discoveries in the lake region. He discovered Lake Nyasa, Lake Tanganyika and Lake Bangweolo. His wife was not able to endure these hardships and died April 27, 1862 in east Africa. He went home to England in 1864 to try to arouse interest in the central part of Africa. In 1865 he left England never to return. The government of England and the Royal Geographical Society supported him meagerly in his projects, but a friend, Mr. Young, gave him more than the two organizations named, had given him.

His chief interest in all of these explorations was to find the source of the Nile and the watershed from which flow the three great rivers of Africa. These matters which are very clear to us now, were a problem and a great mystery to Livingstone. While exploring in the great lakes region, he had his headquarters at Ujiji, on the east coast of Tanganyika. He arrived there March 14, 1869. The next two years he was lost to the world; but after enduring many hardships and facing great dangers, he finally came back to Ujiji, October 23, 1871. By the time he arrived here he was

almost worn out. Not being able to travel, he spent
a great deal of time in prayer and reading his Bible.
He made an entry in his journal, "I read the whole
Bible through four times while I was here." Some one
has very strikingly said that this solitary pilgrim,
whose daily companionship is that of assassins and
slave drivers, never for a moment free from the shadow
of violent death, with shrunken and enfeebled frame,
slowly dying on his feet as he advances or while being borne along by savage hands, yet undeviating in
purpose and with single eye to the fulfillment of the
will of God through his efforts and sufferings, finds his
chiefest solace and inspiration in the Scriptures. This
one fact is worth a whole volume of description of his
opinions and achievements.

He also wrote in his journal while at Ujiji, "I am
a mere ruckle of bones." Dismayed and helpless he
sat down to consider what could be done and what the
next step should be in his explorations. While in this
dilemma his loyal and devoted servant, Susi, came
running at top speed crying, "An Englishman, I see
him," and immediately rushed off again to meet the
stranger. This stranger, of course, was Henry M.
Stanley at the head of an expedition initiated and fi-
nanced by James Gordon Bennett, editor of the New
York Herald. Practically every one thought that Livingstone was dead. Mr. Stanley, who was a news re-
porter, was in Europe at the time. Mr. Bennett cabled
him to go find Livingstone. Stanley wanted Livingstone to go back with him to Europe but he refused.
He wanted another six or seven months to complete
his task of exploration. He even had written in his
journal on June 14, 1872, "I shall complete my task
in March, 1874 and retire."

Stanley lived with Livingstone four months and

"Results of the Gospel in outstation work"

four days. After this stay with him Stanley said, "He made a Christian out of me. Each day my admiration for him grew. His gentleness never forsook him, his hopefulness never deserted him. He had the heroism of a Spartan, the inflexibility of a Roman, and the enduring resolution of an Anglo Saxon. This man has conquered me." After Stanley was not able to take Livingstone to England he left, promising to send reinforcements. These reinforcements came in the form of goods and men on August 14, 1872. A well selected group of fifty-seven men including a young man by the name of Jacob Wainwright, who was trained in the Nassick mission near Bombay, India, came to Livingstone's assistance. We are indebted to Jacob Wainwright for much of the information concerning Livingstone's last days and his death.

After Stanley's departure, Livingstone wrote a letter to Mr. Bennett of the New York Herald, in which he made the following statement: "All I can say in my solitude is—may heaven's rich blessing come down on every one—American, English or Turk who will help to heal the 'open sore' of Africa." This open sore was the enslaving of the natives for commercial purposes and financial gain. We must always remember that when new territory is open, not only the good of missions, but the vices and corruption of men come to the new territory. It is said that Mary Slessor of Calabar, about to sail for Africa, stood on the deck and watched the boat being loaded with casks of liquor for the natives. She said sorrowfully, "Scores of casks of liquor but only one missionary." So it was in the Congo. Liquor and slavery were there, as well as the gospel.

After Stanley had gone back, Livingstone attempted to make another journey. This time he set out

southward toward the great lake region, but they got
only as far as the southern end of Bangweolo. On April
27, 1873, they came to Chitambo village. This is the
last date of any entry in his journal. In this entry is a
prayer of consecration, "I again dedicate my whole self
to Thee. Accept me and grant, gracious Father, that
ere this year is gone I may finish my task. In Jesus'
name, Amen." The next day faithful black men carried him because he was too feeble to walk. They fer-
ried across the river and built a grass hut for him at
Ilala at the southern end of Lake Bangweolo. On the
evening of April 30, 1873, he told Susi, his servant, he
need not stay with him. Susi gave him his medicine
at midnight and left him. In the morning at four
o'clock, May 1, 1873, Susi came to see how he was getting along. He found his master kneeling beside his
cot with his head resting in both his hands, but his
spirit had gone. His black companions took the heart
from his body and buried it under a tree. Then in their
crude way they embalmed his body and dried it. Then
they wrapped the body in calico and bark, and started
on a journey of a thousand miles to Zanzibar on the
east coast. They arrived there February 15, 1874. Three
of the black companions who were responsible for this
journey of nine months were Jacob Wainwright, Susi
and Chuma.

From the east coast the body was taken to London
where he was buried in Westminster Abbey, a fact
made possible because of the faithfulness of his black
companions. His favorite Scripture marks the place
where he was buried,—"Other sheep I have which are
not of this fold, them also I must bring that they may
be one fold and one shepherd." The striking symbols
of an axe and a Bible are carved on the monument in
Westminster Abbey. Livingstone had traveled more

than thirty thousand miles. His chief interest in Africa
was to preach the gospel. Secondarily he sought to explore and to minister as a physician. His work could
be described by three words: abolish—explore—evangelize. The fruitage of his laobrs can be seen in the
fact that a few years after his death, a wave of missionary energy began all over the African continent. The
slave trade was eventually abolished, the source of the
Nile was discovered and commerce was carried on with
the European countries.

Dr. R. J. Campbell, in his biography of Livingstone has given the following description of the effects
of Livingstone's life and work: "On Livingstone's greatness as a missionary and explorer all men are now
agreed. Of the outstanding importance of his contributions to geology, botany, ethnology, there is no need to
argue. Subsidiary though these were to his geographical
discoveries, their value is now universally acknowledg-
ed. The dynamic he communicated to commercial enterprise was in itself enough to establish his claim to
eminence during his lifetime and immeasurably more
since. But far and away beyond all these is the heritage
of his faith in righteousness and brotherly-kindness.
The nineteenth century produced no greater moral
force than he, and its propulsive energies show no
sign of diminution. He has been the means of evoking
more zeal for human welfare, more honest belief in
the capacities of human nature, more unselfish willingness to labour in the cause of human emancipation
from the shackles of hatred, and fear, and hoary an-
tipathies than almost any single personal influence
that could be named; certainly none other has been
more fecund in operation. And the work goes on, and
will go on till the race of man has reached that incon-
ceivable distant goal towards which all the men of vis-

ion of all generations have raised their eyes and led the way."

Dr. Henry Drummond has paid this beautiful tribute to David Livingstone, "Wherever Livingstone's footsteps are crossed in Africa the fragrance of his memory seems to remain. His equipment for exploration and missionary work were his amazing physical endurance, his unconquerable purpose, tender conscience and a soul wedded to Christ."

A monument has been erected close to where his heart is buried in Africa and a memorial mission was established there thirty-four years later by his nephew, Rev. Malcolm Moffat. The following stanza is a fitting close to such a great missionary:

> He needs no epitaph to guard a name
> Which men shall prize while worthy work is known;
> He lived and died for good—be that his fame,
> Let marble crumble—this is Living—stone.

One of the pall bearers at Livingstone's funeral at Westminster Abbey was Henry M. Stanley, who three years before had rescued Livingstone. A few days after the funeral Stanley was in the office of the London Daily Telegraph. Mr. Edward Lawson, the editor, came in and they discussed Livingstone and the completion of his task. Lawson asked Stanley how much needed yet to be done. Stanley answered, "The outlet of Lake Tanganyika is yet undiscovered, we know nothing of Lake Victoria except the little that Speke, the English explorer, has given us. We do not know the source of the Nile River and the west half of the central African continent is still a white blank." Lawson asked, "Do you think you can settle all this if we send you?" Stanley replied, "If I live long enough to do the work it shall be done." A cable was at once dispatched to Mr. Bennett of the New York Herald as to whether he would join in sending Stanley out to Africa to com-

plete the work of Livingstone. The short reply came
back from Bennett. "Yes." Who could have foreseen
what great events would come out of this decision?

In the Autumn of 1874 Stanley returned to Africa
to the eastern coast at Zanzibar. He plunged into the
heart of Africa and after 999 days came out at the
mouth of the Congo River. He then began the further
exploration of the lake region and discovered the
source of the Nile River and also the Congo. He followed the Congo for its nine hundred miles and discovered Stanley Pool in 1876. He continued on until
August, 1877 he came to the mouth of the Congo River.
From there he went back to England and to Belgium.
He gave his report to King Leopold who organized in
1878 the International Association for the Congo. This
association sent Stanley back to the Congo for further
exploration. He went into the interior and made treaties with four hundred native chieftains and established stations along the rivers from 1878 to 1882. To
him must be given much of the credit for opening the
interior of the Congo to missionaries and missionary
societies.

The discoveries and explorations of Livingstone
and Stanley and the information they gave inspired
such men as George Grenfell, Thomas Comber, Mary
Slessor and Dr. Robert Laws to establish mission stations in various parts of Africa. Soon after Stanley's
explorations the English Baptists established stations
from Matadi to Leopoldville and even as far east as
Tanganyika. The American Baptist Foreign Missionary Society was one of the pioneers in establishing
mission stations. Rev. Joseph Clark was associated
with this work. These early missionaries in the Congo
endured many hardships and made many sacrifices in
cpening up the work and doing the pioneering for later

missionaries. In perils of unknown diseases, war, wild beasts, the sea and the jungle; in hunger and thirst, discomfort and loneliness; misunderstood by their own countrymen and suspected by the natives, they cleared places in central Africa where others might build and plant. Between 1879 and 1900 thirty-six missionaries, twenty-eight men and eight women died on the Congo. This included such pioneers as George Grenfell, Thomas Bentley, Mackay, Mary Slessor of Calabar and Colliard of Zambezi.

### CHAPTER VI

# Opening Mission Work on the Kasai River

Of all the missionary societies that established missions in the territory of the Congo or its tributaries, none made as large a contribution to our own mission work as that established by the Southern Presbyterians along the Kasai River in 1891. This work will be discussed at length because of the great help it was to our work and because it was the first mission station in that part of the Kasai territory. The idea of this Congo work had its inception in the mind of Dr. John Leighton Wilson, first secretary of foreign missions in the South Presbyterian church. He had been a missionary in the United Presbyterian church on the west coast of Africa. The General Assembly of 1889 of the Southern Presbyterian church decided to start work in the Congo. The Assembly then called for volunteers for this new work. The two young men who responded were Samuel Norvell Lapsley, a young white man from Alabama, and William H. Sheppard, a young colored man from Virginia. These young men were selected to investigate the field and open the first mission station. Young Mr. Lapsley was the son of Judge Lapsley of Alabama. The judge was not only prominent in judicial circles but also in the work of his church. Since the second young man had much to do with the selection of the field for our work, a more extended history will be given of his life.

Mr. William H. Sheppard was born in Waynesboro, Virginia in 1865. One day while William was playing out in the street an old lady called him into her house and said, "William, I have been praying for you; I have been praying that you grow up to be a good man and some day preach the gospel of Christ in Africa." This experience had a great deal to do with his call to missionary work. In 1883, while he was in training at Hampton Institute, his teacher, Dr. Frissell, came to him one day and said, "Sheppard, wouldn't you like to go to Slabtown with me? We have a little mission work there that the students started." Dr. Sheppard accepted the invitation and there received his first actual experience in missionary work. He also attend ed Stillman Institute for a while, an institution estal lished for the training of colored young people for missionary work. Most of the colored young people in the Southern Presbyterian Mission came from this Institution.

These two young men, Lapsley and Sheppard, set sail in February, 1890 to investigate and finally select a field in the Congo. After they arrived at Leopoldville they went out in various directions from the Congo River trying to locate a field. Finally, they started up the Kasai River and after traveling about a thousand miles they came to Luebo on the Kasai. Here they decided to open mission work in 1891. This was indeed virgin soil. No missionary, Protestant or Catholic had ever been there and the white traders had only recently come to this place. They immediately began to get acquainted with the natives. They had to stay nine months before another steamer would come up the Kasai. They immediately began to get their first words in the native language. They would point out objects and the natives would give the words for the objects. Thus the study of language began at the Southern Presbyterian Mission.

In the first sermon Mr. Lapsley attempted to

preach he emphasized the love of God through Jesus. One woman arose and said, "If we would have known God so loved us, we would have been singing to Him long ago." Ten years later she was one of the leading native Christians at Luebo. After they found the natives friendly they bargained for nine acres for a mission station. Lapsley then planned to go to Boma to see the Governor General and make arrangements for the territory at Luebo. He came to Boma, transacted his business, and then returned as far as Matadi. Here a violent fever attacked him and he died. Dr. Sheppard waited for him but instead of his return, when the steamer came there was a message that he had died. Rev. Lapsley was well liked by the natives. They called him the "pathfinder." He really was, because he found his way not only into this virgin country but into the native's language, their homes and best of all, their hearts. The death of Mr. Lapsley was a hard blow to Dr. Sheppard, who was now left alone until others would come from home; but he carried on faithfully and patiently, and did much in establishing the pioneer work.

In memory of Rev. Lapsley, the Southern Presbyterians bought a vessel for the Kasai, which should be used to transport goods and missionaries between Leopoldville and Luebo. The parts of the vessel were sent to Leopoldville and there assembled. In the year 1904, after making its regular trips for several years, the steamer overturned in the strong current of the Kasai River and one new missionary coming to the field and about twenty-four natives drowned. This new missionary was Rev. Henry Slaymaker. Rev. Vass, who had charge of the vessel, and Rev. Motte Martin also new missionaries, escaped.

Immediately plans were made by the church at

home to replace this memorial steamer, the Lapsley. $40,000 was raised by the children of the Sunday School and Christian Endeavor of the church for the new steamer which was called Lapsley. This new steamer was dedicated December 16, 1905. This was the steamer on which Rev. and Mrs. L. B. Haigh and a number of our early missionaries traveled from Leopoldville to Luebo in 1911-1920.

Dr. Lapsley and Dr. Sheppard came to a territory where the natives had never seen a missionary, or heard a hymn or word of the gospel of Christ. Dr. Sheppard was head of the first colored station in the Congo, that is manned by colored missionaries. The station was called Ibanj. The missionaries labored in this new field on the Kasai River from 1891 to 1895 without a convert. In 1895 the first converts were five young men. By 1906 there were three thousand members at Luebo and one thousand at Ibanj. The Presbyterians were responsible for two and a half million natives. A part of this territory south of Luebo, however, was given to the Methodists, while we received in 1912 a part of their territory west of the Kasai. Dr. Sheppard on his way home from the Congo in 1906 was on the same vessel with Miss Alma Doering, who had been in the Swedish mission along the Lower Congo. Dr. Sheppard told Miss Doering of this large unoccupied field in which they were working. This was an important factor in determining the location of our field.

Dr. Sheppard labored in the Congo until 1910, when because of ill health he and his wife had to return to America. It was at that time that he attended a meeting of the Defenseless and Central Conference representatives and presented the territory along the Kasai. This meeting of our United Board was May 1, 1911 at the Y. M. C. A., Bloomington, Illinois. He was

not only a great missionary among the people of his
own race, but he opposed the cruelty and exploitation
of the Bantu natives by the commercial companies in
the Congo.  This evil was twofold, that of the slave
trade as well as the use of the natives for commercial
purposes.

The period from 1900 to 1910 was one of the sad-
dest and most revolting in all modern history. Reports
came in on every hand of cruelty and exploitation.
Natives were shot or had their hands cut off because
they brought in less rubber than they had been order-
ed by the whites. This crushing toil and brutality became so serious that King Leopold II appointed a commission to investigate the situation. Sir Roger Casement of the British Consul at Boma was chairman of
this commission.  He said that in a district where
there had been five thousand natives in 1887 there
were now six hundred. Villages were diminished
sixty to seventy per cent.  Six thousand people
had their right hands cut off.  Children were
killed with the butts of guns to save amunition.
When this report reached Europe the nations
objected and Leopold II turned the territory over to
the Belgian Parliament. It thus became in 1908 the
Belgian Congo. Some of the missionaries who were
outstanding in their opposition to these cruelties were
Joseph Clark, William Leslie, Dr. William Sheppard,
and Dr. William Morrison. Dr. Sheppard had been offered an American Consulate by President Cleveland,
but refused because he was more interested in his missionary work.

With the death of Leopold II, December 9, 1909, and
the coming to the throne of his nephew Albert I (1909-
1934) the treatment of the natives was much improved.
The new king made a personal visit to the Congo which

helped much in checking the cruelties. The Congo now came under the supervision of colonial governors who made their home at Leopoldville. There were two other factors in relieving the slavery situation. One was a book written by Dr. E. D. Morel on the cruelties of slavery; the other was a commission appointed by King Leopold for investigation assisted by Mr. Casement of Boma. This commission reported in October, 1905 that inhuman treatment was meted out to women as well as men, endless and crushing toil imposed upon them, outrage, murders, whippings freely inflicted. After a study of this report a teacher in the University of Brussels made the significant observation, "An examination of the Congo Free State administration reveals the clear and indisputable fact that the Congo Free State is not a colony in the proper sense of the term. It is a financial speculation. The real aims of those in authority are pecuniary, — to increase the amount yielded by taxation, to exploit the natural wealth of the country, to effect all that can stimulate the powers of production. Everything else is subordinated to this end. The colony is administered neither in the interest of the natives, nor even of the economic interests of Belgium; the moving desire is to assure the sovereign king the maximun of pecuniary benefit."

A great deal of credit must be given to David Livingstone for this opened conscience of the world on slavery. The missions of the Congo met in 1909 at Kinshasha, and objected officially to the injustice to the native and the atrocities committed. Dr. Sheppard and Dr. Morrison's opposition caused their imprisonment for a while. But through a protest by the United States a member of the Belgium Parliament went to the Congo, and defended the brethren and freed them from prison.

Dr. Sheppard's deep interest and sacrificial devotion in the twenty years of service on the field is expressed when he said, "My heart breaks with the unutterable need, the openness of the door, the strategic importance of the present hour. Surely there must be a speedy awakening to the greatness of the need now and to prayer." It is inspiring to read of the self sacrificing devotion of these pioneers in the field of missions. Africa had many great adventurers in its navigators, discoverers, explorers and even its hunters. They were men of courage and accomplished wonders, but the greatest adventurers of all were the missionaries, who felt the call of bringing the gospel to the natives. Such missionaries were Moffat, Livingstone, Mackenzie, Steward, Mackey, Laws, George Grenfell, Lapsley and Sheppard.

But not all the spirit of pioneering and adventuring is to be found in other missionary societies and fields. The Congo Inland Mission Board adventured and had pioneers in its field. The evidences of missionary spirit in the Mennonite church has been within the last fifty years. This is especially true of the Defenseless and Central Conference of Mennonites, who first sponsored our mission work in the Congo. The first missionary interest in the Defenseless church came when money was raised by interested persons, especially Rev. Joseph Rediger, elder in the Salem congregation, for the support of a missionary. This first foreign missionary was Miss Mathilde Kohm, who came from Germany to America and became engaged in city mission work in Chicago. In 1896 she went as a missionary under the Christian Missionary Alliance to the Lower Congo just north of Boma. She was supported by a number of Defenseless Mennonite churches. While home on her first furlough she became a member of the Salem Mennonite church near Gridley, Illinois and was officially supported by the conference as a missionary. On her return to the field in 1900 she took with her Miss Alma Doering and worked under the Swedish Missionary Society in territory between the Congo and the Kasai. Miss Mathilde Kohm was married on the field to Mr. Alvin J. Stevenson in 1904. In 1905 she and Miss Alma Doering returned to Meadows, Illinois.

The first expression of a foreign missionary spirit is found in 1890 when it is reported that one of the congregations gave $90 to foreign missions. In 1898 when the Old Mennonites began mission work in India, leaders in the Central Conference were very much interested. This missionary spirit continued to grow until it began to bear fruitage in 1905. In February of that year a meeting of members from the Defenseless and Central Conference was held at Meadows, Illinois. At this meeting M. S. Steiner, secretary of the Old Mennonites, gave a stirring address on close co-operation among Mennonites in missionary work. This left a lasting impression on the brethren in both conferences and aided in the definite co-operation later on. Definite action in mission work, however, was taken when two stirring addresses were given to both groups by Miss Alma E. Doering and particularly by Mr. Charles E. Hurlburt, secretary of the East Africa Inland Mission on September 14, 1905. The Defenseless Mennonites appointed a committee to confer with the home council of the African Inland Mission in Philadelphia. After this conference it was decided to open a station in the territory of the African Inland Mission.

In 1907 the Defenseless Conference appointed Amos Oyer, Julia Oyer, Anna E. Zimmerman, Alma E. Doering, Marie Schneider (later Mrs. Sywulka) and

Emil Sywulka. Their station was opened at Matara in British East Africa under the African Inland Mission. The churches of the Central Conference also were stirred after the addresses of Dr. Hurlburt and Miss Doering. A meeting was called at the East White Oak Mennonite Church, December 1, 1905. Here a foreign missionary committee was selected and a decision made to send three missionaries. The Central Conference also was to receive stations under the African Inland Mission. The Foreign Mission Committee met at Meadows, Illinois on February 22, 1906. Since there were no volunteers from the Central Conference, they decided to send two young people who were attending Moody Bible Institute, Lawrence B. Haigh and Rose Boehning. They left in April, 1906 for the field. Miss Boehning was married to Rev. L. B. Haigh in February, 1907 at the mission chapel of the African Inland Mission at their central station Kijabe. On April 16, 1907 four more young people were accepted by the Central Conference, viz: Jesse Raynor, L. S. Probst, Laura Collins and Miss Schoenheit. They were sent to the field in October, 1907. After one term of the ten missionaries of both conferences being on the field, they both decided to discontinue their mission work in British East Africa. The Defenseless church recalled their workers from the field. Rev. and Mrs. Sywulka, however, remained. He had been on the field over twenty-five years when he passed away in 1934. He had been of great help to the Old Mennonites in the location of their field in East Africa. Both groups sold their stations under the African Inland Mission. Central Conference gave their missionaries the privilege of staying on the field under the African Inland Mission or returning home. On November 19, 1908 while yet on the field Rev. Haigh tendered his resignation which was as follows:

"Kinyona B. E. A. Nov. 19, 1908.
Dear Mr. Hurlburt and members of the field council,

For months we have been suffering intense pain because of existing conditions in the A. I. M. and we realize that our work has suffered greatly as a consequence of these conditions; and after making it a definite matter of prayer we believe that in order to do our best for God and the most for these benighted souls in Africa, we must sever our connections with the A. I. M. mission and do this day resign from the said mission. Yours sincerely, Lawrence B. Haigh and Rose M. Haigh."

Rev. and Mrs. Haigh returned to the home field in 1909 because of the condition of his eyes and the need of medical attention. It was after his report to the mission board that both Conferences decided to discontinue their work.

Since both conferences engaged in mission work under the African Inland Mission and then discontinued, it may be of interest to the reader to know more about this work of the African Inland Mission. The African Inland Mission was founded in 1895 by Peter Cameron Scott of Philadelphia. The work is located in British East Africa. After a few years the work was headed by Dr. Charles E. Hurlburt, who was secretary and director. His two main convictions concerning missionary work were definite prayer and also definite planning. The society had been granted territory extending nearly a thousand miles to the Nile. The nearest missionary neighbors to the right were one hundred miles and on the left over two hundred miles. Following this line of advance there were no stations hundreds of miles either way. Sir Harry Johnson, a great authority on location of natives, states that this territory was very thickly settled. Dr. Hurlburt's idea of mission work was to place stations about twenty miles apart and make them the centers of mission work in outlined territories. This was spoken of as Paul's method in his campaigning for Christ. Paul established Philippi, Thessalonica and Berea all along the highway; so that those churches might become centers of missionary activity.

This was the idea also of Dr. Hurlburt. He wanted two or three people at each station and a long line of stations several hundred miles long. He also believed that industrial, educational and medical work should be stressed. In other words, that a Christian community should be built up around each station. Kijabe was near the railroad and so was made the general center for all the stations. This was in 1904. It was because of the demand for many workers that Dr. Hurlburt went through the churches presenting this need. There were such large areas of unevangelized territory that many workers were needed. Ex-President Theodore Roosevelt visited Hurlburt's mission in 1910.

It might be that the congestion mentioned as a reason for the discontinuance of our mission work is due to a difference in conception of the method of doing mission work. There are two types of mission work. One is the intensive one where the station becomes the center and emphasis placed not only on the preaching of the gospel but also witnessing to the gospel through educational, agricultural, medical and industrial work. The other method of mission work is entirely evangelistic. The other attempts to reach as many villages and natives with the gospel as possible without being very much interested in building up the Christian community with the station as the cen-

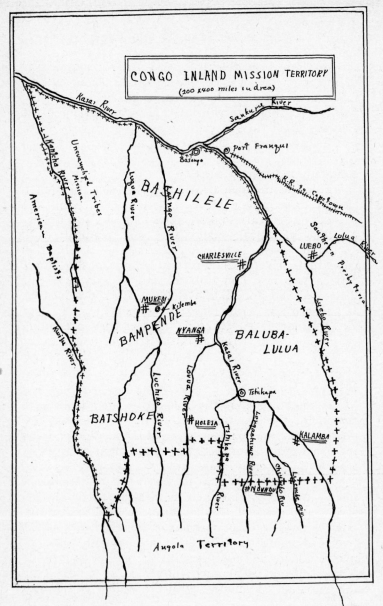

"Charlesville, Mukedi, Nyanga and Kalamba Stations geographically"

ter. It might be well for our missionaries and the Congo
Inland Mission Board to study carefully these two
methods to see which is the most effective in mission
fields. Which one have we used in our territory of the
four tribes?

After the discontinuing of the work in British
East Africa two questions arose with both conferences:
First, what shall be the field selected? Second, shall we
unite our efforts on the new mission field? Letters were
written to six missionary societies to see what were
the possibilities for a new field. The earliest presented
were the Moravian Brethren. But when this proposition was studied it was discovered it was entirely
too large for us to take over. Of the six missionary societies which had been contracted, there were two
which were very seriously considered. One was the
Congo Balolo Mission located south of the upper northern bend of the Congo River. The director of this field
was Dr. Guinness. He was sufficiently interested that
he came from England to America and met with dele-
gates of our two conferences at Meadows, Illinois on
February 24, 1911. He presented the Upper Congo and
gave us an invitation to co-operate with the Congo
Balolo Mission. It appealed very much to the brethren.
Our missionaries were to go on the station, and learn
the language and methods of work. Then we could
select our own field afterwards. The boards drew up a
resolution accepting the invitation. Our missionaries
were to be on the field two years and then have their
own station. This field was as large as the state of Illinois without a single missionary.

The other field seriously considered was that suggested by Miss Alma Doering and Rev. L. B. Haigh
which is located west of the Southern Presbyterian
Mission of Luebo. As stated in the  beginning of this

chapter, Miss Doering had met Mr. Sheppard when she came home in 1906 from the Swedish missionary field. Dr. Sheppard then told her of the great opportunities in that new field. In 1910 after he had returned from the field because of ill health, he again wrote to Miss Doering suggesting this territory. The United Mission Board met and decided to send two representatives to investigate both of the fields and then recommend to the home board which of the two should be selected. The two brethren originally selected were Rev. L. B. Haigh and Rev. Peter Schantz. Since Rev. Schantz could not go, Rev. and Mrs. L. B. Haigh were selected. They left for the field April 15, 1911 and arrived at Luebo September 15, 1911. The rest of the story will be told in remaining chapters.

CHAPTER VII

# Opening Mission Work on the Kasai River by the Congo Inland Mission

Two events of importance marked the beginning of the united work of the Defenseless and Central Conferences in the Congo which finally led to the Congo Inland Mission. The first is the steps by which they were united, and the second is the selection of the field in which mission work was to be done. Ever since Rev. and Mrs. Haigh had returned from British East Africa there were three questions that confronted the two conferences as to their future foreign mission work. The first was whether it was wise to continue work in British East Africa. The answer to the first, as was noticed in the former chapter, was that the work should be discontinued. Both of the two stations manned by the two conferences separately were sold to the African Inland Mission. The Defenseless Mennonite missionaries were recalled and those of the Central Conference were given the privilege of staying on under the Africa Inland Mission or returning from the field. All except Rev. and Mrs. Haigh decided to stay with the British East Africa work. The second question the two groups confronted was whether they should continue mission work independently or should unite their efforts.

Meetings were held by both conferences. The consensus of opinion seemed to be, after prayerful consideration that they should do united work. In both conferences of 1910 held in the latter part of August and the first part of September encouragement was given to united work. January 2, 1911 the Central Mennonite Board of Home and Foreign Missions met at Bloomington, Illinois and two significant decisions were made. One was to send representatives to the Congo to investigate the field and the second to extend a definite invitation to the Defenseless Conference. The following brethren were appointed as a committee: Rev. Val Strubhar, Rev. L. B. Haigh and Rev. Peter Schantz. A meeting of representatives from both groups was held on March 7, 1911 at Bloomington, Illinois. This meeting decided that a united organization should be formed. On March 22, 1911 representatives of the two groups organized and called the new organization the United Mennonite Board of Missions. It was decided to have four members from each group on this new board. The following members were appointed: Rev. Valentine Strubhar, Rev. C. R. Egle, Rev. Peter Schantz, Rev. Ben Rupp, Rev. J. H. King, Rev. J. K. Gerig, Rev. Aaron Augspurger and D. N. Claudon. The following organization was effected: Pres. Rev. Strubhar; Vice Pres., Rev. C. R. Egle; and Secy., D. N. Claudon. These eight brethren were members of this board from 1911 to 1925 without a change except Rev. Troyer took the place of Rev. Augspurger in 19-17; but Rev. Augspurger came back on the board in 1922 in the place of Rev. Peter Schantz. In 1925 the membership on the board was increased from four to five in each group. The purpose of this was to add the two foreign mission treasurers to the board. Bro. S. E. Maurer and Bro. Noah Goldsmith were added. In 19-29 by the new constitution it was decided to have six members of each conference. Rev. Strubhar remained president of the board until 1925, when Rev. E. M. Slagle became president. This board was to have full charge of our work in the foreign field.

The reasons for entitling this book Thirty-Five

Years in the Congo, is because of the significance of the year 1910. It was in this year that it was decided to discontinue work in British East Africa. It was in this same year that Defenseless and Central Conference sold their mission stations to the Africa Inland Mission. In April, 1910 the Central Conference Mission Board decided to accept a proposition made by the Moravian Brethren and it was considered worthy of investigation, but after careful study by a committee it was found that the proposition was entirely too large. In a mission board meeting on August 12, 1910 it was decided to drop this proposition and to recommend that Rev. and Mrs. Haigh go to the Congo to investigate. In the year 1910 Miss Alma Doering and Rev. Haighs were at home on furlough and did a great deal of deputation work throughout the churches of both conferences. The results were seen in the Fall Conferences when it was decided not only to discontinue work in British East Africa, but also to encourage our conferences to unite their efforts in the foreign field. The interest was also evidenced in the money raised at both conferences, several thousand dollars raised in each. In 1910 Rev. Alvin J. Stevenson, who had returned from the Christian Missionary Alliance Field around Boma, now became a member of the Salem Defenseless Church and was ordained as a minister. It was also in this same year that Miss Doering received a letter from Dr. Sheppard and through him we received information about the territory along the Kasai River.

1911 was also a significant year for our mission work. On January 2 it was decided to sent Rev. Haighs to the field. February 24 representatives of the two groups met Dr. Guinness of the Regions Beyond Missionary Society at Meadows, Illinois. On March 7 de-

cision was made to unite the two groups for mission
work. March 22 they were actually united in the new
organization United Mennonite Board of Missions.
April 19 Rev. and Mrs. Haigh left New York for the
Congo. May 1 the new board met Dr. William Sheppard
of the Southern Presbyterian at the Y. M. C. A., Bloomington, Illinois. In September, 1911, Rev. Haighs arrived at Luebo.

In beginning a new work in a new field it is not
only important to investigate the territory, but also to
create interest in the constituency for the support of
such work. To this cause a large contribution was made
by Rev. Haighs and Miss Alma Doering. With their
wide experience in other fields in Africa they could
bring information which developed conviction and
deep interest in our churches. This interest was shown
in 1911 at the August and September conferences when
the Defenseless Conference raised $5800 at one offering
while throughout the year the Central Conference
raised $7000.

As an illustration of this fact there is an interesting article in the January, 1911 Evangel by Rev. Haigh.
In this he discusses the present need from the standpoint of the church. He reminds the mission board that
thus far they have been getting their missionaries outside of the Mennonite Church and that after five years
in service there has not been one young person to
make applicaton for Africa. He asks, "What is the trou-
ble, are you not interested in winning Africa to Christ
or are you not willing to make the sacrifice which
means giving up the thought of becoming wealthy
from your inheritance or profession? What will bring
larger returns in the end than in giving your life in
the hands of the Lord for service in the dark continent?" He emphasizes that preparation should be made

ahead of time. Young people should be trained. The need is for a Mennonite doctor, nurses and men skilled in special lines of work for the African field. It is rather significant that Rev. Haigh in 1910 should emphasize those needs which the mission board has been feeling keenly for these thirty-five years, trained young people from our own constituencies, need of a Mennonite doctor, and men and women skilled in special lines of work.

This far, the discussion has dealt with the preparations for new work in the Congo from the viewpoint of the home church. We shall now follow Rev. and Mrs. Haigh as they go to investigate the field and to establish the new stations. They left with two suggestions made by the board. One was that they should investigate the territory of the Congo Balolo Mission which Dr. Guinness had presented at Meadows, Illionis and then proceed to the new territory suggested by Dr. Sheppard at Bloomington, Illinois, May 1, 1911. The other was that they should report back to the board before final decision was made.

Rev. and Mrs. L. B. Haigh boarded the S. S. Adriatic at New York City on Wednesday, April 19 at 1 P. M. Mr. A. J. Stevenson and Mr. Campbell, missionaries to C. M. A. went on the vessel with them until the steamer left.They arrived in London Friday evening, April 28, where they were met by Mr. Wilkes of the Regions Beyond Missionary Union, who welcomed them to the Harley House. This institution is rather interesting because the Regions Beyond Missionary Society that established it, went to the Congo soon after Stanley's explorations of 1879 to 1883. This society was carrying on very successful work in the Congo in a number of territories. Rev. and Mrs. Haigh stayed in London two months. These were very profitable months. Rev. Haigh attended special lectures at Livingstone College—a medical college for missionaries. Both studied medicine and French by themselves.

Rev. and Mrs. L. B. Haigh

They left London for Antwerp, Belgium where they boarded the Leopoldville on June 29, 1911. On this same vessel were Dr. and Mrs. W. H. Leslie, pioneer missionaries of the American Baptist Society. Dr. Leslie, with Dr. Morrison, Dr. Sheppard and Dr. Joseph Clark did much in bringing about reforms by the Belgium government in more humane treatment of the natives. Rev. Haighs went as far as Matadi by vessel and from there to Leopoldville by a narrow gauge railroad. It is of interest to know that twenty-five years before, this two hundred and forty miles had to be traveled by a caravan of natives. They came to Leopoldville July 27, 1911.

This city, with Kinshasha as the native part of it, is a very important center for the missionaries as well as commercial men. Leopoldville is a political and commercial center. One of the great commercial companies, Lever Bros., the soap manufacturers, is located here. Here the Belgian state officials live. This is also the transport center for goods and missionaries along the Congo and Kasai Rivers. The beautiful Leopoldville is located at Stanley Pool. From here river steamers can again be used for a thousand miles up the Congo to Stanleyville or up the Kasai to Luebo. Rev. Haighs were fortunate in getting passage from Leopoldville to Luebo on the Presbyterian Steamer Lapsley, the story of which has been told in a former chapter. The state steamers at that time were often undesirable because of the rough and uncouth commercial men on them.

Rev. Haighs visited several missions along the way while going up the Congo to Leopoldville. They visited the Christian and Missionary Alliance Mission at Boma as well as the American Baptist at Matadi. They were met at Leopoldville by representatives of the

Congo Balolo Mission. They left August 22 for the
Southern Presbyterian Mission at Luebo in the Kasai
district. This 900 miles to Luebo is navigable. The
Kasai, the largest tributary of the Congo, furnishes
one-third of the water for the Congo River. It is as
long as the whole coast line of Europe. The Presbyterian field is between the Kasai and Sankuru Rivers.

Rev. and Mrs. Haigh remained at Luebo while
making their investigations into the fields westward.
While at Luebo Mrs. Haigh helped out in the school
work. They had an excellent opportunity here, not
only to use Luebo as a base for their investigations,
but also to study the excellent work done by the
Presbyterians. Many of our missionaries have expressed their praise of the work done there and appreciation of the contribution they made to our work
especially in language and medicine. Dr. Morrison's
comprehensive grammar is classic among Bantu Gram-
mars. Their doctors also were of great help at our stations when we had no doctor on the field. This trip
was made through September and October, 1911. The
following is the condensed report Rev. Haigh sent to
the board. He says, "The country we visited lies between Luebo and Kasai Rivers southwest of the mission station of Luebo. This is the district Dr. Sheppard
referred to at Meadows. We traveled along Luebo River south and then west to Kasai River to Kalamba's
village, a distance of about two hundred miles. Kalamba has about 2,000 natives. It is the capital of the
Lulua country. We stayed at Kalamba several days.
When we left, the natives begged us to build a station
there. The natives are anxious for a teacher. This is
always a door of entrance to Christianity. Dr. Morrison, who came to that territory in 1896, recommended
Kalamba. We then traveled north to Djoka Punda and

from there east to Luebo. The Kasai people live in villages with from two to three hundred inhabitants and villages usually from five to twenty-five miles apart." The large central villages, however, are as large as from two to five thousand natives.

Because of the significance of this first trip in this new territory it might be well to give some facts concerning this trip. Rev. Haighs left Luebo, September 27, 1911. They were fortunate in that four natives had happened to come from Kalamba a few days before, whose help they had as guides. The territory into which they entered had been closed to white people until 1909. They had fifty men and boys in their caravan. They followed the narrow winding native paths running through forests, over hills and through valleys. The territory along the rivers is covered with forests and between the rivers are plains covered with a few skraggy trees. The natives have palm trees in their villages. They have a few sheep, goats and chickens, and the native women have gardens. As Haighs approached a number of these villages, the natives hid because they thought they were state men. These state men collect the hut tax from the villagers. Mrs. Haigh was the first white woman many of the villagers had ever seen. Wherever they went the natives pled for teachers. In one village the chief would not let them go until they gave him a paper as a promise that some day they would come to his village to teach his people. It was at Kalamba where they found the largest crowd of natives. As they approached the village three of Chief Kalamba's sons escorted them to the village. They said that Dr. Morrison of Luebo had promised them missionaries.

From Kalamba, Haighs went north and traveled as far as Djoka Punda on the Kasai. Rev. Haigh thought this would be a good place for a transport. Mrs. Haigh in one of her articles gave a significant description when she said that she rode in a hammock part of the way while Rev. Haigh was walking through water several inches deep in the path, and during hard rain while the grass was higher than their heads in many of the narrow paths. "Risking much for the Lord's work." From Djoka Punda they returned to Luebo in October, 1911, having traveled four hundred and fifty miles.

"Some of the first missionary dwellings at the Charlesville Station"

After their return to Luebo Rev. Haigh sent an official report to the Congo Inland Mission Board about his investigations. He stated the following reasons why he thought this field suggested by Dr. Sheppard should be selected. In order to more fully appreciate these reasons it might be well to give a brief description of the work of the Southern Presbyterians up to 1912. As was formerly stated, this work was begun in 1892 by sending two young men, Dr. Sheppard and Dr. Lapsley to this territory of Luebo. By 1912 three stations had been established,—one at Luebo, one at Ibanj, and one at Mutoto established in 1912. The station at Ibanj was one established by Dr. Sheppard and manned by colored missionaries. In 1913 one-third of the native church membership of the Congo was to be found at the Southern Presbyterian Mission, the Congo having 30,000 native Christians and the Southern Presbyterians 10,360. The following missionaries were on the field, one physician, two single missionary ladies, fourteen wives; in all, thirty-three missionaries. They had no converts from 1891 to 1895. In 1896 five young men accepted Christ. This gives us a picture of the large work the Presbyterians were doing when we entered the field.

Just at this time, however, in 1911 they were facing a great need. In the first place, they had charge of 1,700,000 natives in their field, with a limited amount of workers. On the other hand, there were continual demands coming in for teachers. Mr. J. O. Reavis, a Catholic state official, notified Chief Kalamba and others that if they wanted education, they should get it from the Protestant missionaries and by his protection. Daily pleas came from the natives for teachers. One deputation walked 150 miles and told the missionaries that they would put up the building if they would come and teach them. On the other hand, the economic and social conditions were a real challenge to the church. European trading companies were coming in,

attended by all the evil influences that go with them.
The Congo was being flooded with Catholic Priests.
Should this territory have a pagan civilization, or
would the church be able to meet the challenge? It was
for these reasons that the Southern Presbyterians were
very anxious that part of their field be taken by other
missionary societies.  The Southern Methodists took
a part of the field south of Luebo in 1914. They offered us territory west of the Kasai. Three hundred miles
in any direction without a single Protestant missionary, what an opportunity and field for the Congo Inland Mission!  This Rev. Haigh saw and therefore
gave his report accordingly to the board.

The first reason given by Rev. Haigh for selecting
this field was, of course, the large open field without
any missionaries.  There was no congestion here. The
Congo Inland Mission could have its own independent
work. Outside of the Baluba Lulua tribe there was
the Batschoke tribe south of Kalamba, the Bampendi
to the west, and the Bashilele north and south of Djoka
Punda. The second reason was that the Catholics were
not yet in there; and the third that, here definite results could be gotten soon.  This would be an encouragement to the folks at home.  The fourth reason was
that missionaries and freight could be carried inland
on the Presbyterian steamer. Fifth, the work of the
Presbyterian mission had cultivated the  field. Their
influence had gone out far from their stations. This
would be a great help. The last, and perhaps the greatest reason, was the great help we could receive
from the Presbyterian mission.  This help pertained
particularly to two fields: the one of medicine, and the
other of language work. Dr. Morrison's language work
in the fifteen years he was on the field up to 1912 was
of inestimable value to our missionaries.

This report was sent to the secretary of the Congo Inland Mission Board. The board met at Meadows, January 23, 1912. The first act of this board was to incorporate. It was in this meeting where they decided on the official name Congo Inland Mission. They decided that the board pay all expenses on the field jointly; the executive committee on the field should have annual meetings; the executive committee should be composed of the managers of each station; they should elect a president, secretary and treasurer; the duties of this committee were: first, to have charge of all of the affairs of the field, second, to receive new missionaries, third, to assign their field of labor, fourth, to appoint station managers; the president of the committee would be a representative to the colonial government; the secretary should forward a report of the Field Committee to the home board.

Mr. A. D. Campbell at Boma was appointed the legal representative. Rev. A. J. Stevenson, who was on his way to the field, was appointed chairman of the field committee. Rev. Haigh was appointed treasurer and Mrs. Haigh secretary. Rev. Haigh, in his report to the board earlier, had suggested that he did not like to make the final decision of the field alone; so the board decided to send Rev. Alvin J. Stevenson to assist Rev. Haigh in the selection of the field. Rev. Stevenson had done mission work since April, 1896 in the field of the Christian Missionary Alliance in the Congo. He returned in 1909 because of his health. He had married Miss Mathilde Kohm on the field in 1904. They were now members of the Defenseless Mennonite Church. He left New York, February 24, 1912 and arrived in London, March 3. He left on the Leopoldville for the Congo, March 9. He arrived at Luebo, April 29, 1912. He took a Christian native with him from Matadi

whom he had known, to assist him in his work. He left
Luebo, May 2, 1912 for Kalamba where Rev. and Mrs.
Haigh were then located.

### CHAPTER VIII

# Establishment of First Two Stations

Rev. and Mrs. Haigh made their second visit to Kalamba leaving Luebo the second week of February, 1912. There they remained until the arrival of Rev. Stevenson. Rev. Haigh met Rev. Stevenson two hours from Kalamba on May 11, 1912. While Haighs were waiting for Rev. Stevenson to arrive they did some pioneer mission work. Luebo had sent a native Christian teacher to Kalamba and he started a small school. Mrs. Haigh took charge of this school while she was there. She started her work with fifty pupils. In a week's time she had over a hundred. She had women's meetings with as many as twenty women there. On Sunday mornings they had two hundred natives out for the service. Through the week the average was about sixty. Chief Kalamba's sister attended, taking a deep interest in the service. While Haighs were living there they made themselves a temporary hut and the natives built a temporary building for the meetings. The natives begged them to stay permanently.

After the arrival of Rev. Stevenson they started on an investigation tour. They left Kalamba May 20, 1912. They went west from Kalamba and traveled through part of the Bampendi tribe and the Batschoke tribe. They could not make as extensive an investigation as they would have liked because of their handicaps; in the first place, Rev. Stevenson's goods had not all arrived from Leopoldville. In the second place, they had difficulty in getting natives to carry their goods. In the third place, they could not leave Mrs. Haigh alone at Kalamba and an extended trip was too difficult for her. They dipped a little bit into the Bashilele tribe in the far north and then finally came to Djoka Punda.

At this place in our discussion excerpts are given of letters written by Rev. and Mrs. Haigh to the church papers of Zion's Tidings and The Christian Evangel and by Rev. Stevenson to D. N. Claudon, the treasurer, and to Mrs. Stevenson, his wife. These letters are illuminating in the fact that they reveal the real pioneering that was done by our first missionaries. In the December, 1912, Evangel is a report written by Mrs. Haigh on their first days in Djoka Punda. It is now June, 1912, when they are at this station. Their problem was to get a transport station and get it into running order. They selected Djoka Punda because it is the head of navigation on the Kasai River. The rubber company has a transport station close to the river and across the river the Forminere Diamond Company. They wanted to locate near the river so they could hear the steamer whistle. There is a thick forest on both sides of the river here so they had to select their site in the thick forest on the west side of the river. They pitched their tent in a small Lulua village until they had their site cleared. Some of these Lulua people helped them clear the site for their new station. These people were working at rubber and had come from the east. As soon as Haighs were settled Mr. Haigh went back to Luebo to get the goods. As soon as Mr. Haigh returned they cleared a spot and moved out of the noisy rubber village.

On July 23, 1912, just a year from the day they arrived in the Congo the last of their goods reached them. They now began to put up small buildings. The first building was a house to cook and eat in. Then the mud house for dining room and kitchen 12 x 24. The next house to be put up was a bedroom 13 x 13.

In a letter written by Rev. Haigh from Djoka Punda, October, 1912, he says, "We have now been at Djoka Punda three and a half months. We came here with Bro. Stevenson to take steps toward establishing our first light house. Although there were no buildings at the site there was plenty of timber and grass to put up temporary houses. We built our first house with one axe, one hammer and one saw. This house was 28 ft. x 14 ft. and divided into two rooms, a kitchen and dining room. Besides this house we also built a bedroom for us (Haighs), a store house, small hen house and are just completing a temporary bedroom for Stevenson." In a report of our African work sent by Rev. Haigh, January 5, 1913, he reports on Kalamba, where he has been through October 15 to December 15. He built a two-roomed house at Kalamba. Now they have two stations merely started and they long to see them thoroughly manned and the work going along nicely for 1913. They could use six more missionaries. On each station they will need two dwelling houses, boys' houses, store house, and a church building. It will take several thousand dollars to build and equip the stations properly. That is their real need. West is the unoccupied field two hundred miles long and two hundred miles wide of the Bampendi. In the February, 1913 Evangel, Mrs. Haigh in writing to the Ladies Aids makes a plea for clothes for the natives. She says, "You may send us all the shirts, overalls, jackets, vests, handkerchiefs and belts that you want to." Mrs. Haigh has to stay at Djoka Punda until the new missionaries come.

In the messages sent by Rev. Stevenson, the first was on September 7, 1912 to his wife. He said, "We are going to build me a square house 14 feet. It will be built of grass. They have already planted corn, toma-

toes and potatoes. The main food in this district is
manioc. For weeks I have been unable to do anything
but read, write and study. I have committed all to
God. The matter of my health and your coming to the
Congo. His will be done." The second message from Mr.
Stevenson was to D. N. Claudon dated July 25, 1913.
He states that the transport to Kalamba would be very
high the first years but the opportunity to get food was
much greater at Kalamba. They have now definitely
decided to send applications for Djoka Punda and Kalamba. They did not do any more investigating because
Mrs. Haigh was tired out and Rev. Stevenson had
caught a heavy cold which settled on his lungs. But
on the other hand, the Haighs are able to converse with
the people in the Baluba Lulua dialect. And on the
other hand, Dr. W. H. Leslie of the American Baptist
Board, whom Haighs met on the way out decided to
work in the Kwango district. Thus our stations es-

"A typical school building in Congoland"

tablished will be linked in the chain of mission stations from the west coast to Lake Tanganyika.

The latter part of 1912, seemed to be a time of anxious waiting on the part of the missionaries at Djoka Punda. In the first place, they were waiting for a grant from the government for permanent sites so they can begin putting up permanent buildings. The question sometimes arises, which station was first, Djoka Punda or Kalamba? The historical fact is, that if we think in terms of missionary work done, Kalamba was first. But, in official recognition by the government, application for land was made to the government for both stations at the same time, that is in August, 1912. They received information from the government granting permission for temporary buildings by the middle of October, 1912 and Rev. Haigh left for Kalamba, as stated above. Aside, however, from erecting the necessary temporary buildings, while they were waiting they were busy. They had religious services for the natives on Sunday and two or three mornings of the week. Mrs. Haigh also conducted a school but only a few children could be interested. While they were waiting Rev. Haigh went to Kalamba to put up temporary buildings so he and Mrs. Haigh could go there the first of the year, 1913, when the new missionaries arrive.

In the second place, they were anxiously waiting for the new missionaries to arrive. It may be well to introduce the reader to the new missionaries that were to arrive on the field. The first missionaries that were to be accepted were Rev. and Mrs. Aaron Janzen from Mountain Lake, Minnesota. They represented the group of Mennonites now called the Evangelical Mennonites. Several of the brethren from Mountain Lake had attended both the Defenseless and Central Con-

foreign missions. Brethren from the Defenseless Conference and the Central Conference also had attended their conference. Janzens were at Moody Bible Institute when they were appointed by the board January 2, ferences in the Fall of 1911, because of their interest in 1912. In the Congo Inland Mission Board meeting March 31, 1912, Miss Elizabeth Schlansky, Miss Alma Doering and Miss Sarah Kroecker were appointed for

"Before and After"

the field. On April 22, 1912, Walter Scott Herr was appointed. The Janzens and Walter Scott Herr left for the field, November 20, 1912. The three ladies that had been appointed March 31, left for Europe May 24, 1912, Miss Kroecker, to take medical work in England and Miss Doering and Miss Schlansky to study French in France. These two were then to do deputation work in Europe before returning to the field. Miss Schlansky never arrived on the field and Miss Doering returned to America in 1919, after the World War. Miss Kroecker met Janzens and Walter Herr at Antwerp, Belgium and together they left December 7, 1912, for the Congo. They arrived at Djoka Punda, January 24, 1913. Rev. Haigh returned from Kalamba before Christmas, 1912, intending to return with Mrs. Haigh after the new missionaries arrived but because of the illness of Rev. Stevenson plans needed to be changed after they came. Mrs. Haigh wrote that they rejoiced over the arrival of these new missionaries especially Miss Kroecker, who was a trained nurse and could take care of Rev. Stevenson. After the arrival of the new missionaries Rev. Haigh left the latter part of January, 1913, for Kalamba with Walter Herr.

Mrs. Haigh, in an article to the church papers, wrote that Rev. Stevenson is getting weaker very fast. He had contracted a cold by sleeping in a hut which was damp and also by eating improper food, that is not sufficient variety, became very ill. Mrs. Haigh said, she could hear him cough in his hut at night and she never was sure as morning came whether he would still be alive. It had been planned that Mrs. Stevenson should come to the field and that Stevenson should have charge of Djoka Punda and Haighs of Kalamba. But when Rev. Stevenson became very poorly it was suggested he return home. But he loved the work so much that he hesitated to do it. He finally consented that if he was well enough he would go as far as Matadi, and then have a missionary from there go with him. The coming of the new missionaries somewhat revived him but when the newness wore off, he again began to get weaker. He finally lost his voice so that he could only talk in a whisper. Miss Kroecker being a nurse took care of him after she arrived on the field. On Sunday, February 16, native services were held beside his couch in the afternoon. After the service he wanted to sit up. Miss Kroecker put him in his chair. He said he felt very comfortable but while she went to prepare some milk and toast for him and was gone only ten minutes, the native boy came and called her and when she came Rev. Stevenson was already unconscious. He died at 5 P.M., February 16, 1913. Five white men from the Rubber Company made the coffin finishing it about midnight while others dug the grave. He was buried at 10 A.M. Monday.

Mrs. Haigh was practically alone on the station since Janzens were new and did not know the native language. Rev. Haigh had taken with him to Kalamba Mutambo, the older reliable native boy at the station. Mrs. Haigh was left alone with a little nine-year-old reliable boy Tumba. Mrs. Haigh had to have charge of the services. She conducted a native service in the Baluba language. She spoke on the parable of the Rich Man and Lazarus, showing the difference between a Christian's death and a sinner's death. Rev. Janzen then conducted a short German service at the grave. His texts were John 5:24-30 and Deut. 32:29.

For the rest of the description I will give it in the words of Mrs. L. B. Haigh. "The only long boards we had were of a box in which a wheel chair came, which our new workers brought with them, of which his coffin was made. We lined it with a sheet, putting excelsior under the head for a pillow. We dressed him in his white suit, then decorated the body with ferns and roses. We miss our dear brother; his chair at the table is vacant. His place on the field is empty. Who will fill it? Is there not some one at home to take his place? His grave is here to show where his body rests. The memory of him lingers to tell us of the sacrifices made for the Gospel's sake. We pray that his death may not discourage any one. But much more lead many young

The resting place of Rev. Alvin J. Stevenson

people to give themselves to God, for these people, for whom this dear brother lay down his life. Repeating his own words to Sister Kroecker, "Don't get discouraged because I am sick, you don't need to get sick too; even though I should die, don't let it discourage you, for people die at home too." Though we urged him often and plead with him to go home or to go see a doctor, for we knew a doctor would order him home, while he was still strong enough to undertake the long journey, yet he preferred to stick to his post, feeling he was needed here. May this same spirit prompt many young people at home to realize that they are needed on the battlefield against Satan and his great forces. Our hearts ache for our dear Sister Stevenson and her dear children, who have been so anxiously longing to see their papa again. We are praying that God may comfort them, as He alone can. We know that you will do all you can for the beginning of your work in Africa."

Rev. Stevenson was born December 23, 1879, in Canada. He came to U. S. in 1890, made his home at Lowell, Massachusetts. He united with the Baptist church. He attended the Christian Missionary Alliance Training School in New York in 1894. In the spring of 1896 he went to West Africa under the C. M. A. He returned in December 1899 for his first furlough. His wife died while he was on the field in 1902. In 1904 he married Mathilde Kohm, who was in West Africa supported by the Defenseless Mennonite Church. Rev. and Mrs. Stevenson came back on furlough in 1910. He united with the Defeneseless Mennonite Church at Gridley in February, 1911 and was ordained as a minister. He was sent to the Congo in February, 1912, where he died February 16, 1913.

Some great missionary has said that in the early history of practically every mission field there is a grave to suggest the sacrifice that is made for the spread of the Gospel in foreign lands. Brother Stevenson is the only one of eighty missionaries under our

board that died on the field. There are a number of
our missionaries who, as Paul said, "have been nigh
unto death but the Lord spared their lives." There
were some children who died on the field. Rev. Janzens lost two children, one in April, 1913, a small baby
only nine hours and the other, their boy Sonny, who
was born November 18, 1914, and died June 28, 1919.
There may have been other children of missionaries
who died on the field of which the writer has no knowledge. But Brother Stevenson's death reveals first of all
that spirit of sacrifice and pioneering that was necessary in those first years and the other, that spirit of
courage which faces hardships without fear of complaint.

The death of Rev. Stevenson also made it necessary for the Congo Mission Board to reorganize on the
field. Rev. L. B. Haigh was appointed chairman and
Walter Herr assistant. Rev. Haigh returned from Kalamba to Djoka Punda in April, 1913, which left Brother Herr alone at Kalamba. Rev. Haigh made a brief
trip into the Bashilele tribe found fifty miles south,
seventy-five miles north and a hundred miles west of
Djoka Punda. He found them very friendly and re-
ceptive. Rev. and Mrs. Haigh began to study the Bashilele language hoping that they might do something for
the tribe soon. In the latter part of 1913, it became
necessary for Rev. Haigh to go to Matadi and Leopoldville to make arrangements for transport of cargo.

In a letter of Mrs. Haigh written November 8,
1913, she gives a schedule for a week's work at Djoka
Punda. At six thirty A.M. Rev. Haigh has a service
in the chapel for the working men. Breakfast is at sev-
en thirty. Rev. Haigh spends his time supervising the
native workmen, in the men sawing boards, doing
carpenter work, chopping down trees, underbrush and

vines, clearing the ground and getting gardens ready.
A lot of salt must be kept on hand for rationing the men.
Rev. Haigh needs to look after the business end of the
station. Mrs. Haigh has a school every day in the week
except on Saturday from ten to eleven. Then every-
body rests until two o'clock. At two the language classes are held for missionaries Kroecker and Herr. These
two also take care of the garden and towards evening
they visit villages until dark. At six thirty in the evening they again have school. On Sunday at two o'clock
they send two boys out to gather the natives together
for a service.

One of the very reliable sources of information for
the writing for this part of the history is found in the
interesting and informative annual reports give by
Rev. Haigh to the Congo Inland Mission Board. These
reports were made available through our church papers for the benefit of the constituency. On January 24,
the arrival of Janzens, Kroecker and Herr. In the first
part of February Haigh and Herr go to Kalamba. The
death of Rev. Stevenson, on February 13. In April a
little baby born to Janzens but died after nine hours.
In June, a baby named Lawrence born to Haighs. After Haighs return Brother Herr became very sick and
the station was left in the care of the Christian native
Mutoto. The station was without a white person from
March to June when Janzens arrive. Rev. Haigh says
that at the close of the year 1913, we are much more
comfortably situated than a year ago yet there is much
to be done. We have temporary houses at each station
for three missionaries, a chapel and a store house. At
each station is a department where logs are made into
lumber by the natives. Rev. Haigh makes a plea for
machinery from America to help them in this work.
They are ready to build permanent buildings. In evangelism three evangelistic services are held. They need

to prepare native workers to send out to the villages. The final and perhaps one of the most important events of 1913 was the grant by the government of land for the two permanent stations Djoka Punda and Kalamba. This was in August, 1913. A cable was received at Washington, Illinois giving this information while the Central Conference was having its sessions there.

The work of Miss Alma Doering in Europe was beginning to show results. A number of candidates from different countries in Europe are making application to the board to go to the Congo. Two of these accepted by the board and left for Africa, July, 1914, were Oscar Anderson and Frederick Johnson. Brother Anderson knew Greek and French. He interested the natives by his stereoptican views of the Holy land. He and Bro. Johnson were stationed at Djoka Punda. The following review is given by Rev. Haigh for the work of 1914. As stated above Johnson and Anderson arrived. The effects of the first World War are felt very keenly both in the passage of missionaries and in the sending of money. Miss Doering was not able to secure passports to leave Europe because of the war. In September, 1914, Rev. Haigh and Dr. Anderson visited Luebo. July, 1914, Miss Kroecker went to Kalamba. Rev. Haigh then continues his report as follows: Djoka Punda had to be located in a sparsely settled territory because it had to be near the Kasai River for transport. But after two years of labor there has been a marked increase in school from twenty-four to sixty-eight. The average attendance at Sunday School is seventy-five. There are sixty at the week day services. Medical treatment has been given to 843 in a year. A new church is to be organized in the beginning of 1915. Ten members from Luebo have moved to Djoka Punda and the station has two converts. The average attendance at Sunday preaching at Kalamba has been 208 and Sunday School 216. School attendance is 126. 825 received medical treatment. Three out-posts have been established. Two have native teachers and the third a teacher is sent from the station. They have now built a permanent dwelling worth $1,000 to the mission. Goods that come to Djoka Punda must be carried by natives to Kalamba. At Djoka Punda they have found clay which can be used for brick.

In the year 1915 three new missionaries arrive on the field. Henning Karlson, Miss Anna Meester and Miss Elsie Lundberg. These are European missionaries sent out by Miss Doering. They arrive on the field March 18, 1915. The other is that Rev. Haighs, who are urgently in need of a furlough, leave Djoka Punda in May, 1915. Before Rev. Haigh left he baptized the first two converts of our own Congo Inland Mission work.

## CHAPTER IX

# Our Mission Work from 1916 to 1926

As we come to the year 1916 a number of changes took place in the missionary personnel. While Rev. Haighs were on their furlough, Miss Sarah Kroecker, who had been working at Kalamba, became the wife of Dr. Oscar Anderson and together they worked at Djoka Punda. They left the field permanently in November, 1916 to work under the Swedish Mission Board where they are still laboring today. Practically all of the European missionaries served only one term or less. Frederick Johnstone left the field in April, 1917. Henning Karlson married Elsie Lundberg and then left the field in June, 1918. Two new missionaries came from Europe, G. Tolefson of Norway, and Edgehart of Sweden. They served only ten months and then left to work at the Luebo station. Miss Meester of Holland left in April, 1918 for another field and later became the wife of a state physician. We have in these, "so many one term missionaries," the fact stated by Rev. Haigh in the beginning of the work, that permanency will depend on selecting our missionaries from our own constituencies.

Rev. Haighs returned to the field in March, 1916. With them came Rev. and Mrs. J. P. Barkman and Miss Agnes Sprunger for their first term of service. These three missionaries are now serving on the field, (1945) and have the longest terms of service of any of our missionaries. Rev. and Mrs. Aaron Janzen and Walter Scott Herr left the field in July, 1916. Walter Scott Herr resigned in 1917 and Janzens did not return to the field until January, 1919.

A review of the work for 1916, reveals the following facts; Rev. Haighs arrived on the field May 19 and in July Janzens and Herr left for home. It was decided at the annual meeting that Barkmans should go to Kalamba and Miss Sprunger remain with Haighs at Djoka Punda. Rev. Haigh states that the year 1916 was the best year of the mission since its beginning. He says there are few missions in Africa that have had such a promising outlook. In three years' time they have six native teachers caring for outstations and ten other places where school is held three months of the year. At each station there is a training class for native Christians. The work that is being done in the villages by native teachers is showing results. They now have over a hundred in their services. Twelve natives were baptised and received into the church. It may be of interest to know that among these were three women,

A group of native teachers, "Miracles of the Gospel"

the first women converts on our field.

As we come to the end of the year 1916 our mission work is growing out of its pioneering state in the period of youth. Practically every phase of our mission work which is being done today finds its origin in these beginning years of our pioneer work. In these years the two stations were built up with permanent buildings, outstations were established, a training school curriculum was developed, natives became Christians and churches were started.

Missionaries today in our field will never know what were the trials and hardships of these early missionaries with all the handicaps they confronted. To Rev. and Mrs. Haigh must be given a great deal of credit for the pioneering in these years. It required courage, patience and a great deal of Christian love to assume the leadership in those days. Missionaries came from various countries of Europe and from our country with different ideals and different interpretations. They had never worked together before and then to confront this new and hard situation in this virgin land and a trying climate was a task which no ordinary man could accomplish. Rev. and Mrs. Haigh served faithfully and served well and today, in their declining years, and Mrs. Haigh's serious illness, they need our sympathy and prayer and our thanksgiving for what they accomplished as pioneers in the Belgian Congo. In a personal letter to the writer Rev. Haigh writes as follows: "While I was writing down these facts concerning our foreign missionary work I could not help but feel impressed with the fact that something ought to be done to preserve the early history of the mission which only Mrs. Haigh and myself are thoroughly acquainted with. It will be intensely interesting and useful if ever a complete history of the mission is written in future years. I could not but help and feel that I would enjoy going back to the field some time and gather some data from natives who knew something of the conditions at the early beginning of the mission. When I think of some of the changes which have taken place it seems hardly possible. Only the first missionaries first on the field can know the hardships of the beginning of a mission in a country like Africa, or the real pioneer work." Rev. Haighs returned to the home land in June, 1920. After a few year's service as pastor at Danvers Mennonite church, Danvers, Illinois, they moved to North Carolina where they now reside.

In the year 1917, Rev. and Mrs. Emil Sommer came to Djoka Punda as missionaries. They left New York, July 12, 1917 and because of the dangers in traveling on the high seas their vessel took the southern route to try to avoid mines. They came near to the coast of South Africa, Cape Town, when their vessel struck a mine and was sunk. They were rescued in a boat and after some dangerous experiences they finally landed on the coast of Cape Town having lost all their belongings except the clothes they wore. They finally arrived on the field, October 25, 1917. Their arrival was very much appreciated by the few missionaries that were left on the field.

As we watch the developments of the mission work on the two stations there are two outstanding facts. One is that the mission station becomes the center of the missionary activities of that territory. Here native Christians are to be trained and then sent to the outlying villages to become teachers. Since the village becomes such an important factor in the mission program, it is well to understand what a Congo village is like, because villages in the Congo are not the same as

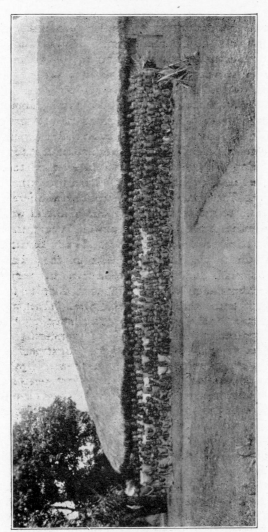

"A teacher and some of his converts"

villages in our country. An interesting description is
given by one of our missionaries. These Congo Villages are scattered out according to the tastes of the
people, on a prairie, on a hill or in a valley and surrounded by tall grass, bush or forests. Some of these
villages may be large as Kalamba, having about 2,000
natives but most of them have from two to three hundred and are built from ten to twenty-five miles apart.
The school is one of the most important institutions in
these villages. After the natives came in contact with
white people they had a great desire to learn to read
and write. They attributed the mysterious power of the
white man to the fact that he could read and write and
so they wanted to receive this power. In fact, the desire
of the native for teachers wasn't always because they
wanted the gospel but rather because they wanted to
read and write and do arithmetic. But this very desire
to gain knowledge becomes an open door to the missionary to teach and preach the gospel. When we think
of the schools of the villages established by the missions especially in the days of our pioneering, we can
not think in terms of our modern educational system.
All Mrs. Haigh had to teach the natives at Djoka Punda was an old torn chart and five first readers. The
teacher becomes his own architect of the school building and with the help of his pupils builds it. They have
no desks and use small logs for the seats. This building is often used for church services as well and is
built at the expense of the natives rather than the mission. And yet with all of these handicaps the report
shows that eight hundred children and young people
were taught daily by native teachers at the villages
where the two missions had established schools. Besides this, in 1917, there were three hundred who were
taught at the two stations. The native Christians are

trained at the mission stations and are then sent out as the teachers to the surrounding villages. This is a very hard task for the native Christian. They are often several days journey away from the mission and so are very much alone. The missionaries at this time were not able to visit them as often as they should have been visited because of the scarcity of the workers. In this discussion of the native Christian teacher, the missionary describes the difference between the heathen natives and those that are Christians which is a great tribute to the power of Christianity to transform life. First of all, he is a higher type of native than

"A native Christian worker and his family"

these to whom he goes to teach, he has been accustomed to having plenty of food, a good house to live in, and being with people who are willing to some extent to assist him in whatever way possible. Upon arriving on his new field of labor he finds quite a different state of affairs, he is introduced to a poor excuse of a house—only a hut—which is alive with insects of all kinds, and

told that he is at the place where he is to live. Naturally, he builds himself a better house before he has been
there long. Next he finds that the poor people are
merely existing, living on the smallest quantity of food
of the poorest quality. There are no large gardens of
bananas, plantains, manioc, corn, sweet potatoes, millet, etc., such as he has always seen, but instead there
is only a small patch of manioc. When the meal is
ready it is only a few sticks of boiled manioc while at
home a nice round loaf of manioc bread was always
set before him, with greens or meat to eat with it. Now
he really suffers from hunger at times, he must pass
through the same experience as the people whom he
has come to teach. The poor, smoky, insect-ridden hut
does not affect him as much as the hunger which he is
called upon to endure. Yet these young fellows plod
along without much complaint. Our hearts can not
but help to sympathize with them when we visit their
villages and see with our own eyes the conditions just
as they exist.

In a letter written May 20, 1918, to the home land,
Rev. E. A. Sommer gives a description of some of the
work done by the missionaries on the Djoka Punda
station. We have three services on Sunday, every
Tuesday and Friday prayer meeting at six A.M., also
Wednesday evening at seven. School every morning
from nine to eleven-thirty A. M., and from one-thirty to
two. Bro. Haigh has a teacher's training class every
afternoon from three to five, where the native teachers
receive special training along doctrinal lines. Some of
these teachers have been holding out-posts, they were
called in for a short time for this special training. We
have a number of outstations which are manned by
native teachers. We also have a women's sewing class
every Friday afternoon; boys' sewing class every

Tuesday afternoon; dispensary work every evening. From five to six P. M., we have school for the workmen. We have thirty workmen on the station. I suppose you wonder what we do with so many men. In the first place they have been accustomed to work only when they felt like it and that was very little, allowing their women to do most of the work.

We also have from thirty to thirty-five boys which we call fence boys. They are constantly on the mission compound. These boys are clothed and fed by the mission. They are taught to read, write and work, with the one great aim uppermost and foremost in mind, that is, "To teach them the things of God." We feel that this is one of the golden opportunities in the mission work to get the boys while their hearts are yet young and tender and are not tainted with all kinds of superstition, sin and vice. These boys, before they came in our care were never taught cleanliness nor manners, and when they came to us one sometimes wonders where the possibility lies. Many of them show a great change in a short time, while others make very slow progress. You can imagine this number and type of boys takes no little care, and one sometimes is at his wit's end just what to do.

We now come to the last annual report made by Rev. Haigh before he left the field or in the beginning of the year 1919. As they looked back they rejoiced at what God had accomplished through the missionaries and the Christian natives and the teaching and preaching of the gospel. There were many disappointments and testing times but many of them were "growing pains" produced by the rapid growth of the work. The native church had now increased its membership to sixty. Rev. Haigh remarks that there could have been four times as many if they would be interested only in membership, but they wanted to be sure to accept only those who had really accepted Jesus Christ as their Saviour. Then there came the great problem of discipline of these young Christians. Coming out of a religion of fear and ancestor worship and pagan environment it becomes very difficult for the native Christian to remain true to the teachings of Christ. But even when they backslide many are willing to come and repent and to be again in fellowship with their Saviour.

One of the outstanding institutions established at Djoka Punda in 1917 was a training school in which it was planned to give a two years training course to those who are to become teachers and evangelists. After the two years of training they will be sent out to remain permanently in the villages. The school opened with six students and during the year eight others were added making fourteen. This does not meet the great demand for teachers that comes to the stations. But considering four years ago when they had only one teacher, and he poorly trained, and now have thirty outstations cared for by eighteen native workers it after all marks great progress. As they enter the year of 1919, changes have come about in the missionary personnel. All of the European missionaries left and there are only five missionaries on the field, Rev. and Mrs. L. B. Haigh, Rev. and Mrs. Emil Sommer, and Miss Agnes Sprunger. Rev. and Mrs. Barkman had to come home in August, 1918, because of Mrs. Barkman's health. In 1919, however, there came to the field Rev. and Mrs. Janzen bringing with them three new missionaries; Rev. and Mrs. William Kensinger and Omar Sutton. Bro. Sutton was sent to take charge of the industrial work.

Another new type of work developed at Djoka Punda was the girls' work. When the first missionaries came to the field they had a vision that some day they would establish a girls' home at each station. This vision was realized in 1918. Not only does this work get the girls away from evil influences but it means the training of Christian women to become the wives of the native Christian men.

Another event of importance in the year 1919, was the establishing of a new mission station in a new tribe. Djoka Punda and Kalamba are both in the tribe of the Baluba-Lulua. Soon after the Haighs arrived on the field Rev. Haigh made an investigating tour into

"Does it pay to send the Gospel?"

the Bampendi tribe from Kalamba. A number of such tours were made from 1912 to 1919. The missionaries had written to the board several times asking that they might open a new station. On January 4, 1918 the Congo Inland Mission Board at its meeting decided that a third station should be opened. Rev. Haigh states in a personal letter that in August of 1919, he met a government official at Nyanga's village for the purpose of selecting land for a mission station. Rev. E. A. Sommer accompanied him on this trip. The station was officially opened in 1921. The official sanction for the opening of the station was given at a Congo Inland Mission Board meeting July 5, 1920. Rev. Janzens were placed there until they left the field in November 1921.

A few years after Rev. Haighs were on the mission field Mrs. Haigh's mother, Mrs. Dorothea Boehning willed $500 to be used for the building of a church at the station where her daughter would be located. This building was to be constructed by Rev. Haigh. By 1919 the time had come when brick could be made and such a building could be erected. The $500 with the accumulated interest of $160 was sent to the field to build. The bricks were made and carried on the shoulders of the natives up a long hill to the chosen spot where the church was to be built. The iron was ordered from England. In April, 1920, the ground was broken and the foundation laid for the first brick building ever built at Djoka Punda or now called Charlesville in honor of Prince Charles of Belgium. The walls were built of brick three and a half feet high and brick pillars extended up to support the roof. The space above the wall is reserved for ventilation. The church has a seating capacity of six hundred. The size is ninety by forty with a twenty-eight inch diameter bell. Back of the pulpit is a room for prayer meeting and special classes. It was the finest and most substantial church building for hundreds of miles in every direction. The dedication took place the first Sunday in August, 1921. There were five hundred in attendance that day.

One of the problems which faced the Congo Inland Mission Board in 1920 was missionaries. As stated before, Janzens resigned in May, 1921 and left the field. Rev. Haighs left the field in June, 1920 and did not return. In August, 1920, Barkmans returned to the field bringing with them two new missionaries, Miss Alma Diller and Miss Amelia Bertsche. In November, 1921 Lester Bixel went to the field.

The year 1921, was marked by an increased program both in money and missionaries. In this year through the influence of Miss Alma Doering, the North Danvers Mennonite Church, a congregation of the Central Conference pledged to raise $10,000 in five years for the work in the Bampendi tribe. This was to be paid $2,000 a year. The other part of the program was the addition of an auxiliary to the Congo Inland Mission Board called the Grand Rapids Auxiliary. This meant an increase in the constituency from which money could be received and also an increased number of missionaries to be sent to the field.

In February, 1922, Miss Agnes Sprunger returned to the field for the second term. In November, 1921, Rev. Emil Sommer and in July, 1922, Mrs. Emil Sommer. The year 1923, however, marked the time for the sending of the largest number of missionaries in the history of the Congo Inland Mission. Through the Grand Rapids Auxiliary and the Congo Inland Mission Board there were sent out in February, 1923, ten missionaries: the Mosers, Klopfensteins, the Valentines, Miss Alma Doering, Miss Theresa Gustafson, Miss Emma Rickert and Miss Weith. In May, 1923, Miss Erma Birkey. In October, 1923, Rev. and Mrs. B. F. Langdon came to the field. In November, 1923, six were sent to the field. Kensingers returned second term, Miss Clio Briggs, Beckers, Miss Beulah MacMillen; thus making a total of nineteen missionaries sent in 1923. This same year the fourth mission station was opened at Mukedi in the Bampedi tribe. At the close of this period of 1926, Rev. I. R. Detweiler of Goshen, Indiana, became the secretary, treasurer of the Congo Inland Mission Board in place of D. N. Claudon who had held this office from its beginning.

Another change which took place was the resignation of Miss Alma Doering who went to another field. Also the return of Rev. and Mrs. William Kensinger to the home land because of the health of Rev. Kensinger. The Grand Rapids Auxiliary also definitely and finally separated from the Congo Inland Mission Board to organize a new society called the Untouched Tribes Mission with Miss Doering as field secretary and deputation worker. After the change of the business office to Goshen, Indiana and the return of Rev. Kensinger, he was appointed as assistant to Rev. I. R. Detweiler. The office now began to send out the Mission Monthly with up-to-date information about the field.

## CHAPTER X

# Mission Work In the Congo 1927 to 1930

Great changes came about in the Congo from 19-12-1927 both in the general civilization in the Congo as well as the mission work in our field. This change is well expressed in a letter written by Rev. Lester Bixel to the Congo Inland Mission Board. He states that the work at Djoka Punda is getting not easier but more difficult because of the change that has come about in the environment of the natives. A civilization without Christianity has come in with commercialism in the last few years. The natives are plunged into a new environment. Old needs are met in a new way. They seem to be perplexed. The traders, the priests, the missionaries, the diamond men have all come in at the same time. This has changed the native outwardly but only the gospel can change him inwardly. They have left off some of their old customs but the things that they have learned from the white men are more sinful and destructive than their own customs. It also hardens the native to the gospel of Jesus Christ. This condition in the Congo is true throughout Africa. Mr. J. H. Oldham after traveling through British South and East Africa said that, "we are living in a fool's paradise if we think that missionaries can maintain their present influence in Africa with the changing environment. Missions are, relatively speaking, at a standstill compared with the other influences, economic, political and social which are changing the whole life of Africa. This is no need for discouragement but it presents a challenge. Every crisis is an opportunity. The church in the home land and the missionaries must move forward with faith, vision and courage if they wish to maintain their position and become leaders in the Congo."

The establishment of the new mission field of the Untouched Mission Tribes left the station at Mukedi without any white missionaries. The missionaries located there were either at home on furlough or went over to the other mission. In order to meet this crisis and challenge, Henry Mosers offered to return to the field before the end of their furlough. They set sail with Miss Agnes Sprunger and Miss Theresa Gustafson, June 25, 1927. They arrived on the field August 18, 1927.

One of the problems which faces every mission board is to keep in as close touch as possible with the missionaries on the field. This can be done by careful study of the field and a continual correspondence between the missionaries and the board and the constituency. But other mission boards have discovered that the most effective method is to send some one from the home church to the field. The missionaries had been asking for this ever since 1916. In the Congo Inland Mission Board meeting in 1920 a resolution was passed recommending that someone be sent to the field from the board but for reasons which are not known to the writer no one was sent. In 1922 the board again discussed favorable the sending of a representative. In 1925 the missionaries not only asked but practically demanded that some one come. By 1928 the board at home began to take definite steps to send some one to the field. The particular incentive in 1928 was not only to visit the field but also to attend the West Africa Jubilee Conference in September, 1928 at Leopoldville. The Congo Inland Mission Board met at Goshen, Indiana, June 19, 1928. The regular routine of business was transacted. The following missionaries were accepted for the field of Africa. Miss Erma Birkey to sail the latter part of June, Mr. and Mrs. Amie to sail August 11, and Mr. and Mrs. Becker to sail some time in November. The most serious consideration at the board meeting, however, was the sending of a member of the board to Africa. This representative to be sent was to spend considerable time in visiting other mission stations, to attend the Jubilee Conference and then to visit our field. Two resolutions were passed at this meeting. One was that we favor sending a member of the board to Africa. The second was that Rev. Emanuel Troyer should go providing his church gave its consent to release him. Rev. Gerig of Chicago and Rev. Detweiler of Goshen were appointed to meet the First Mennonite Church at Normal where Rev. Troyer was pastor, and to present these resolutions. It was the hope of the Congo Inland Mission Board that the constituency would see the significance of their action taken.

After it was reported by Rev. Gerig and Rev. Detweiler that Rev. Troyer was not able to go, the question as to who should go became serious. In the latter part of June, 1928, Rev. Allen Miller wrote a letter to Rev. A. M. Eash relative to other matters but incidently referred to the fact that he heard that Rev. Eash had been asked to go. Rev. Eash replied stating that he had not been asked but that he might consider going if it were the wish of the Mission Board. Rev. Miller then visited Rev. Eash and presented the matter and also wrote to Rev. Troyer who informed Rev. I. R. Detweiler, secretary of the board. Rev. Detweiler then, as secretary of the board asked Rev. Eash to go. Rev. Eash, being a member of the Central Conference,

a meeting was held on Monday, July 23 at the home of Rev. J. H. King of Carlock, Illinois. The following members were present at this meeting: Rev. Allen Miller, Rev. Emanuel Troyer, Rev. J. H. King, S. E Maurer, Rev. Raymond Hartzler, Rev. W. B. Weaver and Rev. A. M. Eash. At this meeting it was decided that we favor sending Rev. Eash and that we ask for a meeting of the Congo Inland Mission Board. This meeting was held at Goshen, Indiana on Thursday, July 26. Here it was officially decided to send Rev. Eash to the Congo to investigate the field. He was also chosen as field secretary of the board. He was ordained to the office of Elder by Rev. Emanuel Troyer, Sunday, August 12, 1928 at the 26th Street Mission. He sailed from New York City, August 16. He left Antwerp, Belgium, August 28 on his way to the Jubilee Conference at Leopoldville on the S.S. Elizabethville. The first valuable experience that came to Rev. Eash was the meeting of about ninety missionaries and missionary representatives going to the Kinshasha Conference. While on the way to Kinshasha Rev. Eash had the privilege of visiting the Christian Missionary Alliance Mission north of Boma. He also visited the mission at Matadi.

The West Africa Conference held at Kinshasha registered one-hundred and ninety-one persons representing sixteen missions in the Congo, six other West African countries, Great Britain, United States and Belgium. Of the one hundred and ninety-one, one hundred and forty-four are Congo missionaries. Miss Erma Birkey was the only representative of our Congo Inland Mission stations except the field representative, Rev. Eash. Some of the subjects that were discussed at the Kinshasha Conference were the education of the native, the indigenous church, the medical work, land, labor and government, literature, industrial and agricultural and evangelistic work.

A part of the program of the field representative was to visit the work of some of the thirty missionary societies in the Congo in order to get ideas and suggestions which might be of value to our own work. Several missions had been visited before he came to Leopoldville. After the West Africa conference, Rev. Eash traveling with a party of missionaries going up the Congo, arrived at the Disciples Mission at Bolenge. This place is located directly on the Equator. This was the oldest of the Disciples Missions, having been opened in 1898. It is one of the most progressive missions in the Congo. They have evangelistic, educational, medical and industrial work. This mission had over 20,000 native Christians, four native ordained pastors, six hundred and fifty native teacher evangelists. The church is seventy-five per cent self supporting, self governing and self propagating.

After leaving Bolenge Rev. Eash went on to Stanleyville visiting with missionaries from a number of different missions and stopping at two Methodist missions. The last one of the stations visited outside of our own field was the Southern Presbyterians from whom we had received so much help. Concerning the work at Luebo, Rev. Eash states that on Sunday morning he sat in church with 1200 natives present and at least 800 others meeting in four other buidings. There were 982 in Sunday School in the afternoon.

After having had contact with the work and workers of twenty-three different organizations he states a number of impressions concerning missionaries which bears worthy consideration. The first was the personality of the missionaries from the viewpoint of train-

ing as well as character. The most effective gospel after all which the missionary preaches is that which
is revealed in his own life. Another observation concerning the missionaries was their support. It was
discovered that those that are better paid are better
able to equip themselves for the task before them. A
third observation was the interesting one of the missionary's relationships to the board, to each other on
the field and to the natives. The final observation is
that practically all the societies are denominational
missions. A mission may be denominational and still
practice the spirit of unity, fellowship and co-operation
with other missionary societies and missionaries.

In order that the reader may get a better idea as
to what was the program of the field representative before he arrived at Charlesville, the following report is
given from his correspondence: "Since arriving at
Boma on September 12th a total of sixty-eight days
have passed as follows: twenty-three days in travel,
twenty-eight days visiting missions, seventeen days attending conferences. The mission stations visited
were at Bolenge and Coquilhatville (Disciples); at
Tunda, Wemby Nyama and Minga (Southern Methodist); Mutoto and Luebo (Southern Presbyterian).
These visits were four or more days in length and were
supplemented by shorter stops at American Baptist,
British Baptist, Swedish Baptist, Congo Bololo and
Westcott Brothers Missions. During the traveling days
I was never without the company of missionaries or
other secretaries who had a common interest with me.
In the twenty-three days of travel I covered 2822 miles
as follows: 1487 miles on the Congo and Lualaba Rivers by steamer, 450 by train, 25 by hammock, 75 by
bicycle, 785 by automobile. 110 of the miles traveled
by auto were at night without lights on the car, the
remainder in quite a variety of types of vehicle and

varied degrees of comfort."

Rev. Eash arrived at Charlesville, November 19, 1928. He had now attended the West Africa Conference

A royal welcome for Rev. Eash

and had visited other missionary societies and is now ready for the third part of the program to visit the stations of our own field. He states in a letter that he believes that his eight weeks of visiting other missions has been of even greater benefit than those received at the Kinshasha Conference. It is, however, to be noted that the discussions at the West Africa Conference served as a basis for his experiences in visiting the missions.

The plan for visitation at the four mission stations was as follows: He is to visit Charlesville three weeks during which time a trip of investigation will be made into the Bashilele tribe, then he would go to Nyanga for a few weeks and then go on to Kalamba to be there during the Christmas holidays. During this time he and Mr. Barkman will make a trip into the Batschoke tribe. Then finally, he would go to Mukedi and be there for the Annual Conference in January after which he would leave February 1, 1929 for the home land.

In order to give us a picture of the work that was being done at our mission stations by 1929 the writer wishes to quote from a report given by Rev. Eash of the work of the Barkmans at Kalamba station. Concerning Rev. Barkman he says, "He is director of the school work. Yesterday there were three hundred and twenty-five in attendance. There are twenty classes and all the teaching is done by native teachers. The pupils are taken through reading, arithmetic, writing and spelling to an equivalent of about seven grades of our schools. He is pastor of the church and has charge of all the activities. On Sunday morning there were 1,-185 in the service, with five hundred in the afternoon Sunday School. Then there is the evening Young People's service, converts' class twice weekly, a class in

A class in "black and white"

catechism every week evening but Saturday, choir practice two evenings in the week, chapel two mornings at six o'clock, the outstation work to supervise and the pastoral attention that needs to be given to two hundred baptized Christians. On the 27th of December, forty-one were given water baptism. In addition to this work he has the industrial work of the mission. He has just completed a new brick carpenter shop and has some other building that needs to be done. The furlough of Mr. and Mrs. Becker who have been due back for more than a year, has left Mr. Barkman the only American man at the mission. Fortunately he has a number of native Christians to whom he has delegated many of the tasks so that he is able to carry on—but he needs help very much. The mission cannot afford to allow our missionaries who are old in experience and who are willing to do double work, to be worn out as is being done here at Kalamba."

A summary of a report given on Nyanga. "Nyanga has a very beautiful location—something like Mutoto of the Presbyterians and Minga of the Methodists. It is on a high hill with a fine outlook. They need no mosquito nets—which is rare for missions. They do not have a spring for water, the soil is rather poor and the distance to clay is rather great. The population is rather sparse but they have a large area from which to draw. The native built church in the days of Misses Briggs and MacMillan and the boys' and girls' buildings have been built without using mission funds. The native village in which the mission natives live is being built up by themselves instead of by the mission as is practised in some places. The life there is possibly a little more closely supervised than is good for the natives.

Distribution of work. Bro. Enns — Evangelistic work and the small boys; Mr. Amie—Industrial work and the older boys; Mrs. Amie—Office, translation, mission village, transport; Mrs. Enns—Two babies, school; Miss Unrau—Medical, girls. I should have said there are fifty girls in the mission girls' building, about sixty small boys and about forty older ones."

The last letter written by Rev. Eash, January 15, 1929, is from Mukedi station and near the close of the Annual Conference of the Congo Inland Mission. Rev. Eash commends the missionaries and the missions for the splendid work they have been doing. Fourteen of the eighteen missionaries were in attendance and all were enthusiastic about their work. The statistics showed that there had been an increase in the enrollment of children in the outstation and mission schools and a general growth in all the activities. The church membership was steadily growing and larger responsibilities were being placed on the native Christians who showed leadership. The particular point emphasized by Rev. Eash was the attitude of the missions on the development of the native Christian church. Year by year the four stations have been placing larger and larger responsibilities on the native Christians as deacons, assistant pastors and treasurers.

Rev. Eash returned home from his trip to the Congo in May, 1929. The Congo Inland Mission Board held its regular session at Goshen, Indiana, May 27, 28 at which time Rev. Eash gave a very voluminous and instructive report of his survey of the work at the four stations presenting the problems of each station and his reactions in his conference with the missionaries. He presented a number of recommendations which were discussed and acted on by the board.

The question which we hear so much today was raised many times by various individuals. "Was this trip necessary?" We very wisely ask the question because today (1945) the Congo Inland Mission Board has

Missionaries and Guests, "workers together"

again decided to send a representative to the field. The
fact that this involves rather heavy expenses, more so
today than in 1928, makes it important to consider
whether it is of sufficient value to justify the outlay
in money and time. These questions can best be answered by the fruitage of such an adventure. It is very
certain that the contribution made by Rev. Eash was a
large factor in the progress of our mission work and its
effects can be felt even now.

The first definite benefit to be noted was on the
field. A number of the missionaries wrote home ex-
pressing their thanks and appreciation for the representative sent to the foreign field. One of the missionaries said that he saw more in the few months he was
there than many of them see in a term of service. His
suggestions and constructive criticism were of inestimable value to the work of the field. Second, it was of
definite value to the Congo Inland Mission Board because it gave them information and interpretations
concerning the work on the field which could not have
been given any other way. In the third place, it stimu-
lated the interest in missions in the constituency. Rev.
Eash was selected by the board as field secretary to
visit the churches, locate candidates for the field, to
enlarge the constituency for support of the work and to
promote the spirit of stewardship throughout the
churches.

The final result was the decision made by the board
to print a missionary magazine called the Congo Missionary Messenger. This magazine was to be an organ
of the Congo Inland Mission Board to bring information to the constituency. The purpose of the paper was
stated in the following words: "There is an urgent need
for some organ through which to bring to our constituency a more effective report of the needs on the field

and of the work that is being done." The first issue of this magazine was issued in August, 1929. The Congo Missionary Messenger was to become an avenue through which the constituency was to understand better the cause and task which the Congo Inland Mission had accepted. First, the task to make the Congo known to the home folks. Second, to tell the story of how the light of the gospel came to the Congo people through the transforming power of the gospel of Jesus Christ. So the message of this missionary magazine was to bring the gospel as the only remedy in the Congo; to present the cause of the indigenous church; and to promote programs and activities that would produce fellowship and co-operation looking to an African Christian Church.

As we come to the close of the year 1930 the following report will be of interest to the reader. The membership of the church in the four stations, eight hundred; number of catechumens, six hundred and seventy-five; converts in the year, one hundred and thirty-eight; church attendance, one thousand, nine hundred and seventy; average attendance at the station schools, six thousand six hundred and seventy-five; enrolled in training classes, one hundred eight.

As we come to the end of the pioneering period and establishment of our four stations (1911-1930) it might be well to state the plan of this history of our work in the Congo Inland Mission. Much of this work has been discussed at length because very little is known by the constituency concerning the beginnings of our work both from the standpoint of our Congo Inland Mission Board, our missionaries or our field. As years pass fewer and fewer records would be available for the writing of such a history. We are fortunate in having a few of our earliest missionaries with us today. Rev. and

Mrs. L. B. Haigh live at Roseboro, North Carolina. Mrs. Haigh has been an invalid for a number of years. Rev. and Mrs. J. P. Barkman have just completed their fourth term of service in the Congo and are due for a furlough. Miss Agnes Sprunger is completing her fourth term. Rev. and Mrs. Emil Sommer are now at Pulaski, Iowa.

The discussion of the Congo Inland Mission work from 1930-1945 will be briefer and will be rather a summarizing of the work done by each station. It is not because we feel that the work is not as important or that the missionaries are not making a large contribution at the present time or are not doing a splendid work, but rather because the present day history can be found in the Congo Missionary Messenger and through our church papers. The pioneering work in the early days should always linger in our memories and should give us inspiration and encouragement in our present day activities. May we always cherish the memories of those that have gone before.

### CHAPTER XI

# Charlesville—Djoka Punda Station

The territory which has been assigned to the Congo Inland Mission Board has four mission stations, ranging in distance apart from sixty to two hundred miles. Two of these stations are in the Baluba-Lulua tribe and two in the Bampendi. The territory is about two hundred by four hundred miles—some fifty million acres of land—with a population of about four hundred thousand natives. For this the Congo Inland Mission is responsible. The two other tribes namely, the Bashilele and the Batshoke have no main stations in them. They do, however, have a number of outstations.

The purpose of this chapter is to give a brief history of the station called Charlesville or Djoka Punda in the Baluba-Lulua tribe. The station was called by its native name, Djoka Punda until about 1927 when it received its English name, Charlesville. This name was given in honor of the son of King Albert of Belgium, (1909-1934) whose name was Charles.

It may be well to recall the early history of this station as has been recorded in past chapters. In October, 1911 Rev. and Mrs. L. B. Haigh, after having been at Kalamba for quite a while went north along the Kasai River and came to Djoka Punda. They considered this a very good place for a transport station as well as to do missionary work among the Bashilele tribe. They, however, waited for the arrival on the field of Rev. Alvin J. Stevenson before the final decision was made. Rev. Stevenson came to Kalamba May 15, 1912 and soon after he with Haighs left for Djoka Punda. He agreed with Haighs that this was a good place for

transport. August 30, 1912 Rev. Haigh applied to the
government for Djoka Punda. Just one year later,
August, 1913 the government officially granted it. During this year the forest was cleared and the first temporary buildings erected. It was during this same year,
February 16, 1913, Rev. Stevenson died at this station. The first missionaries at Djoka Punda outside of
Haighs were the arrival January 24, 1913 of Rev. and
Mrs. Aaron Janzen, Walter Scott Herr and Miss Sarah
Kroecker. Our past history records the rapid progress
of the missionary work at this station. Some marks of
progress are that in two years and a half the school
grew from four to sixty-eight and there were as high
as seventy-five at the week-day preaching. By the end
of 1914 eight hundred and forty-three medical treatments were given. In January, 1915 the first two converts of the Congo Inland Mission were baptised and
the first native church organized with twelve members, ten coming from Luebo. Year by year new phases
of Christian activities were introduced until by 1930
the following departments were definitely established.
The evangelistic, educational, medical and industrial.
Besides these at Charlesville there was printing and
the development of literature and itinerating work.
The progress of the work from 1930 to 1945 can perhaps best be shown by reports from the field and statistics in the various departments of work.

The first, and probably the most important of all
of the activities at the mission stations, is the evangelistic. This is indeed the ultimate goal of the work of the
Congo Inland Mission. As a final result of all of its efforts it hopes to produce genuine Christian men and
women. Its hope is that these may be genuinely transformed by the wonder working power of God through
Christ that they will radiate His life in all their relationships. All of its activities are planned to con-

tribute to this one end. In order to realize this goal the mission has given itself to the fourfold task of living the Christ life before the African, preaching the simple gospel of Jesus Christ, conducting a ministry of healing for the many who are sick and diseased, and training and developing a native Christian body that can eventually be made the perpetuating agency in spreading the gospel message. This group is the African Christian Church. The ultimate goal is to make this indigenous church self supporting, self propagating and self governing.

The home church sends the missionaries to the field to do this work. The missionary travels the long distance to Africa; he exposes himself to the climate and diseases of a tropical country; he spends his time and energy in many details of the work which in themselves are often questioned as being not directly evangelistic; he reduces languages to writing; he writes school books; he translates Scriptures; he administers medicines; he builds houses; he cultivates fields; he teaches in the schools; he encourages more sanitary living in home and village—there are a thousand things that he finds himself doing in order that eventually he may be insured from the native a ready response to the appeal to forsake sin and accept salvation through Jesus Christ. All the work of the missionary is ultimately evangelistic.

Out of the many examples of the transforming power of Jesus Christ there is this striking one which is an outstanding reason for mission work. In the year 1916 at Djoka Punda among a group of workmen on the station was one by the name of Songamadi (Yosefe Songamadi). In 1917 this young man was baptised by Rev. L. B. Haigh. He was in the special class conducted for the purpose of teaching reading, and writing to the workmen. From there he entered a special teacher's class and received special traning for Christian work. In the fall of 1919 he was sent out as a village teacher and was used mightily of the Lord. Although he was a member of the Baluba-Lulua tribe he was sent as one of the first teachers among the Bampendi. He acquired the Kipende language very rapidly.

When our missionaries first made a survey of the Bampendi tribe they took Songamadi along as interpreter. This took him away from his village of Chief Kalangonia. The missionaries returned to Charlesville and left Songamadi alone. After many bitter experiences there, in opposition from the natives, he established a school numbering about forty boys. This was in 1920 and was the real beginning of Mukedi.

He had now come to the age when he wanted to get married so he went back to Charlesville and from there went from village to village to hunt a wife. His intended wife came to the Nyanga station and after six months accepted Christ and was baptised. Her name was Beneka. When the Mukedi station was regularly opened in October, 1923, Songamadi became the teacher of the Kipende language to the missionaries. The greatest test of this great Christian native came in the summer of 1927. Some of the missionaries at Jukedi had gone home on furlough and the rest went to work under other mission boards. This left Songamadi and his wife alone in sole charge of the entire station and its activities. In spite of the taunts and abuses of the native villagers he remained true at his post from May to September, 1927 until the Mosers came to the field. This is what the gospel of Jesus Christ can do for natives in the Congo.

Two of the activities connected with the evangelistic work are the outstations and the itinerating work. Itinerating has two definite objectives, one to become acquainted with new territory, villages, and tribes, and the other to select villages as outstations for evangelistic and educational work. As has been stated before, the Congo Inland Mission is responsible for nearly 400,000 people in four large tribes. Nearly half of these are found in two tribes in which we have no permanent stations manned by white missionaries, the one being the Bashilele and the other the Batshoke. The Bashilele has an estimated 60,000 natives while the Batshoke has 150,000.

The itinerating which has been carried on since 1911 in our work, results in the establishment of out-stations. The purpose of these outstations is very well described by the field secretary in 1932. The Congo Christian Church has an effective testimony for its Lord. In addition to the large work being done on the four mission stations under the close supervision of the missionaries, there are about two hundred centers scattered over that vast territory in which native Chris-tian men with their families are stationed. These Christians who have themselves been saved out of dark paganism are devoting their entire time to telling the gospel story to their fellow men. In each of these evangelistic centers the Christian man in charge is both teacher and preacher. On week days he conducts a village school five days a week for nine months of the year. Every morning he gathers the villagers to the chapel for a season of worship and on Sundays he conducts Sunday School and preaching services. The attendance in these village schools averages about fifty and larger groups attend the preaching services.

God has richly blessed this ministry of the Congo Christians and today in many of these outstations small groups of believers have come out of their pagan-ism and are sincere followers of the Lord Jesus Christ. Many others are enrolled in the catechism classes in

Congo Christian, consentrating in class work

which they are taught the fundamentals of the Christian faith. At the end of 1933, over 4900 were enrolled in these catechism classes in the almost two hundred villages. Itinerating again becomes necessary to supervise these outstations.

In the missionary conference held at the Mukedi station January 9-15, 1929 during the time of the Field Secretary's visit to the Congo, the Evangelistic Committee adopted the following policy concerning the outstation work. 1.—The aim of the outstation work shall be threefold: a.—In the first place it shall be evangelistic through the preaching of the Word, the singing of gospel hymns and catechical teaching. It shall be an avenue for making Christ and His work of salvation known to those of the villages that cannot easily be reached by the station services. It is hoped that through this evangelistic effort many may find Him as their Saviour. b.—In the second place, this work shall be educational. The simple rudiments of reading, writing and arithmetic shall be taught in the day school. This will fit the pupils to read the Word of God for themselves and to better know its messages. c. — Another great purpose of the outstation work is the task of discovering in the villages those who have the larger leadership possibilities. These shall be brought to the main station and trained to become leaders in the evangelization of their own people, and in building up the native Christian church.

2. — Supervision: a. — The outstation teachers should be visited at least twice each year. b.—The purpose of the visits should be to inspire the teachers and pupils to greater efforts. Criticisms should be given in a sympathetic and helpful manner. The visits should be made spiritually helpful and uplifting. c.— The supervision shall consist in: 1.—Testing the pupils as to school work, as to catechism, as to readiness for

baptism, as to aptitude. 2.—Keeping in touch with the teachers; see that they respect state etiquette, have sufficient plantations and properly built and equipped houses and chapels. 3. — The outstation school and vacation months shall correspond with those on the main stations. A teacher shall be subject to discipline if he takes a vacation during school terms.

The following letter by one of the missionaries at Charlesville as reported in the "Twenty-five Years of Mission Work in the Belgian Congo" describes the practical work done in these outstations. "How beautiful are the feet of them that preach the gospel of peace and bring glad tidings of good things!" Romans 10:15. We are thankful to God that as a result of many years of work, there are some sixty-six evangelists of Charlesville station who are out in various villages proclaiming the unsearchable riches of Jesus Christ. They all have the sunshine of Christ in their hearts and are endeavoring to lift their own people out of the miry clay with the power of the gospel and have Christ put new songs in their hearts. We thank the Lord that these evangelists have the Sword of the Spirit, the Word of God, which is able to direct them in the paths that our Master has trod.

From time to time these evangelists have been selecting good Christian boys and girls from their own village schools and sending them to the Mission or station school for further instruction. On an average there are about 85 boys and 35 girls who live on the mission compound. These boys and young men are in training to be future evangelists, where as a rule the girls become wives of the evangelists and great helpers in women's work. All of these children attend the station school with the other village children. The average attendance of the station school is about 300, and here it is where special emphasis is placed on religious instruction including the catechism. After attending for some time, they can well understand those precious words of the Psalmist in Psalm 119:11, "Thy word have I hid in my heart, that I might not sin against thee." The teaching staff consists of about eleven teachers whose business it is not only to teach school, but to be soul winners as well.

One of the most encouraging works at Charlesville is that of the Evangelistic Department. There have been times of disappointment and times of great rejoicing, but we thank the Lord that there is a steady growth. The main objective of the mission is to make the native church an indigenous one. At present (1937) there is an assistant pastor, five deacons, sixty-six outstation teachers, and a total church membership including that of the outstations of 2,184. One of the most encouraging phases of this department is that of the Christian Workers' Groups, who go out on Sunday afternoon to near-by villages, some of which are ten miles away, to preach, sing, witness and testify of the good things that the Lord has done for them. Then the same Sunday night they gather in the church to give an account of their meetings as well as of the offerings taken. How they rejoice with one another and we with them as they tell about the number they had at the meetings, those who have accepted Christ as their Saviour, and those whom they had a hard battle with and requested the prayers of the Christians so that the Lord might give them victory over Satan.

How we thank God for the faithful Christians in Africa. They are not only an example to their own people but often to us and teach us many lessons. A number of converted Christians have been studying the catechism of the mission under the direction of our outstation teacher and requested us to baptise them. We tested each one of the candidates for baptism by asking them many questions as to their belief and those who successfully passed were baptised. One evening we started to test an elderly woman and she seemed to be quite nervous and afraid, and as a result she failed miserably. We told her that we were sorry that we would not be able to baptize her until she had absolute conviction that she was saved and knew Jesus Christ as her Saviour. She was sadly disappointed, arose, and told us that she was going home to pray all night and wrestle with God as Jacob did of old, and that she wanted us to test her the following morning. She believed with all her heart that God would give her victory and would help to convince us that she knew Jesus. The next morning she came back with determination in her heart and a victorious smile on her face. Upon questioning her again, it did not take much to convince us that she prayed through and as a result she was baptised.

While visiting in the villages, visiting our Christians, I heard some one singing a hymn. Walking in the direction of the singing I saw one of our Christian mothers holding a young child in her arms and singing that song, "Trust and Obey." Upon coming to where she sat, I noticed that the child was not living, but dead. What a heart touching scene. I often wondered whether my faith would hold out in such a dark hour. There were no heathenish dancings at that funeral, no lacerations of the body, no nakedness, no drunkenness, but just a few Christians, and that song never to be forgotten in my memory, "Trust and obey, for there's no other way, to be happy in Jesus but to trust and obey." We thank the Lord unceasingly that He has permitted us to be ambassadors and laborers with Him.

The next department in our missions which is bearing great fruitage is the educational. The native has a great desire to learn to read and write. He feels that the secret of the white man's power lies in his ability to read and write. So from 1900 to 1911 down to the present time natives come to the missionaries begging that they send teachers to the native villages. The primary purpose of this is not always a hunger for the gospel but a desire for knowledge. Knowledge to the native means power. The great opportunity for the missionaries is the fact that the Belgian government has left the education of the native very largely to mission schools. By 1930 various phases of educational work were carried on. The village schools were established in the outstations with Christian natives as teachers. Bible stories, memory work and gospel songs were part of the curriculum. Teachers' Bible training classes were established. Translations of the Scriptures were made in the native language. The printing of proper literature for the natives in the villages was encouraged. One of the missionaries gives the following report besides direct teaching and preaching in the schools we have other means of spreading the gospel. Sunday Schools are held at the main station as well as most of the outstations. Prayer meetings are held one night of the week. Special children's meetings are held at Charlesville. Christian Endeavor societies have been started and choirs organized. In a report of 19-37 the following facts are given concerning the educational department of Charlesville.

Today in the constant seeking everywhere for more wisdom of various kinds, we rejoice that in the Congo we can still preach, "Christ the wisdom of God," the true wisdom, that which will last throughout eternity. It is a great joy to us that in our school work we can give a large portion of time to the Bible teaching. How long we shall have this privilege we know not; but we are so happy that we can still teach the blessed Word and exalt Christ in our schools. Our grade school averaged an attendance well over 300 throughout the year for which we are thankful. Some of our students walked a distance of more than 15 miles round trip to school regularly and had to cross a large river which took a great deal of time too. Their interest encouraged our hearts. We began four new regional schools. At three of these schools students study until they have completed the first part of the grade school course, and then if they are called to the Lord's service they are to go to the fourth school which we call the preparatory school for Bible school, which is located about ten miles from Charlesville where they complete their grade school work and take a Bible course in preparing for entering the Bible school at Charlesville. After which they come to Charlesville to the Bible training school for Evangelist-teachers.

Rev. E. A. Sommer, who went to the Congo in 1917 and served there until 1932 gives a fine description of the work of the school at the mission. The Congo Inland Mission has four educational centers in which about four hundred boys and two hundred and fifty girls, ranging in ages from six to sixteen, under the careful supervision and instruction of the missionary and native leaders, receive their Christian and religious training. About eighty per cent of these children come from our outstation schools which are conducted by our trained native Christian leaders. These children are usually hand picked and are the most promising pupils of our outstation schools.

When these children enter these educational centers they find everything so different from the pagan village life that it seems like a new world to them. They are housed in large dormitories where tribal distinction has no preference and where sanitation and punctuality are strict rules. Great care is exercised to throw about them the most wholesome Christian influence

and environment, with the great objective of leading
them to an acceptance of Jesus Christ. In their development in the school life any sign of ability in leadership
is carefully cultivated, for out of this group of pupils
come our future students for the Teachers' Training
Classes, where they receive the special Bible instruct-
tion.

Not all who enter our dormitories in these educational centers find their way into the teachers' training school for special service, but as they go back to
their own villages as Christian young men and women
they are a great asset in building up the native church
and establishing Christian homes in their home community.

Apart from their school hours and recreational
periods, the boys have various jobs about the station
and the mission fields and plantations. The girls have
their own dormitories which are quite apart from those
of the boys. These are carefully supervised by a missionary lady and a responsible native chaperon. Our
boarding schools for girls are making a good start in
giving the little girls a chance to live a happy girlhood
life.

It is the pagan custom to keep women on a lower
level than men. Our work among the women has always encountered greater difficulties than it has among
the men. Pagan chiefs and men in common are very
often opposed to the emancipation of girls and women.

At our stations the larger portions of the forenoon
is devoted to school work and the afternoon to practical
activities when the girls are divided into different
groups for various kinds of work. The practical work
given to the girls is such as will fit them to, in the future, be efficient wives, capable housekeepers, good
mothers and worthy examples in Christian womanhood. Since ninety per cent of our girls after finishing

their school training marry the graduates of the Bible
School, we exercise great care so that their training
is such as will fit them to take their places in the
schools and in religious activities with the women.

One of the definite goals for educational work outside of raising the general level of intelligence is the
training of future leadership. To realize this result calls
for a force of native Christians with sufficient training
to enable them to efficiently fill the leadership positions. Out of the graduates from the station schools
the choice young men and women are selected and giv-
en several years of additional special instruction in
preparation for this work. This advance instruction is
in Bible Pedagogy and associated subjects.

The primary emphasis in these training classes is
in strictly theological subjects, however, there are also
lessons in elementary carpentry, agriculture, first aid in
medicine and hygiene. The instruction in carpentry
deals with the making of simple furniture such as is
needed in the native home, it not being the purpose of
developing thoroughly trained industrial men. The
purpose of the training class work is to develop teachers and evangelists. However, we want evangelistic
men who can use their hands as well as their heads,
and who can preach the gospel of labor at the same
time as they are proclaiming the supreme gospel.

The courses are as follows: Bible Doctrine, Pastoral Theology, Homiletics, Church History through
the Reformation, Typology, Synthetic Bible Study,
Analysis and Personal Work. The Bible School is the
heart and center of all our evangelistic work, and those
people in the home land who support the students
while they are in training, will through the supported
students be preaching and teaching the gospel, as they
go out from the training schools to the outstation
work.

The school has a high spiritual requirement and every effort is made to ascertain if the students are really in earnest and are developing into truly good soldiers of Jesus Christ. After the first year in training, the students have week end assignments for preaching and teaching. Thus they are putting to practice what they have learned. These appointments are to districts where there is no messenger of the gospel. Hundreds of souls have been won to Christ through the efforts of the students. The school's influence is felt far and wide.

One of the heartening evidences of genuine religion in these native people is the fact that, even though the government and local trading companies afford remunerative positions for natives who have been in mission schools, these young people choose rather to work in the mission where they can devote themsleves to propagating the gospel of Jesus Christ.

Another department which has been rendering a large service in our mission work is the medical. From the very beginning we have been fortunate in having practical and trained nurses on the field. They have rendered valuable service in the ministry of healing. But the outstanding need through all of our work has been the doctor. Rev. Haigh, in 1910, suggested that some Mennonite young man should prepare himself to be a doctor in the Congo. Repeatedly the missionaries not only suggested, but requested that a doctor be sent. The mission board made repeated efforts, but without success. Finally the board succeeded in getting Dr. Rudolph Unruh, who was on the field from September, 1931 to March, 1936. From this time to November, 1942 we were again without a doctor until the arrival of Dr. Merle Schwartz. Charlesville, however, has been quite fortunate in having the Presbyterian Mission at Luebo so near at hand. Their physicians and hospitals have been of inestimable value. The need of a doctor is great from the standpoint of the health of the missionaries but even greater, as a practical and effective medical evangelist. This is interpreted clearly by Dr. Unruh when he says, "From the experiences that we have had in the Congo just how practical and effective is medical evangelism? Let me just briefly tell you what we have done in the way of evangelism in connection with the medical work. All evangelistic services and work were similar at the various stations where we had the clinics. You must remember that I stayed at each one of the stations for about six months before we located permanently at Mukedi and where we built the hospital. The first definite attempt that we made was at Charlesville where we began with the regular services in the morning before the medical work began. This was in the hands of the deacons of that station and they did very good work. At this station we also began with the leper work and with the

A general view of the Charlesville Station

evangelistic work among these people. They were treated as clinical patients twice weekly and each time they came for treatment on the days that such treatments were given the deacons held evangelistic services with them. These proved more effective than any that we had after that. The deacons reported that a number had definitely decided to become Christians. The leper work at Charlesville had to be given up because of lack of medicine and so we lost track of these people.

This history of the work of the Charlesville station will be closed with the 1944 statistics furnished by the station. The station reports the following: number of missionaries, 7; native helpers, 2; assistant pastors, 5; deacons, 1; church members at the beginning of the year, 4434 and at the end of 1944, 4757. The number of outstation teachers, 137; professing Christians awaiting baptism, 1137; the average attendance at Sunday morning church and Sunday School, 1026. In the Bible training class 52 boys are enrolled. In the educational department, the following report is given: native boys at the station, 36; native girls, 23; the number of regional schools, 12; rural schools, 131; the number of teachers in the regional schools, 30; in the rural schools, 150; in the station schools, 18. The school attendance in the regional schools, 6120; total in all of the schools, 6990. Some estimate of the medical work done at the station is revealed by the following statistics: native medical helpers, 3; medical patients, 1340. The printing office furnished literature for the four stations. In the agricultral department twenty-eight acres of ground are cultivated during the year. The following missionaries have served at the Charlesville station since the time it was established. Haighs 1911-1920, Stevenson 1912, Frederick Johnstone 1914-1917, Oscar Anderson 1914-1916, Emil Sommers 1917-1926,

Rev. Sommer 1930-1932, Kensingers 1919-1925, Suttons 1923-1937, Rev. Sutton 1919-1922, Lester Bixels 1920-1930, Grabers 1930-1945, Russell Schnells 1932-1945, Roy Yoders 1935-1945, Aganetha Friesen 1938-1945.

### CHAPTER XII

# Kalamba—Mukenge Station

The second station of the Congo Inland Mission is in the Baluba-Lulua tribe, located near Kalamba village called the Kalamba station. The station received its name, as has been noted, from the chief of the village of about 2,000 natives. This territory around Kalamba was a part of that given to the Southern Presbyterians in 1891 when they began their work. This village is located in the particular territory referred to by Dr. Sheppard in his meeting with the Congo Inland Mission Board, May 1, 1911.

Rev. Haighs arrived in Luebo in the latter part of August, 1911. The first investigation made after their arrival was into the territory between the Luebo and Kasai Rivers southwest of the mission station of Luebo. They traveled about two hundred miles until they came to Kalamba's village. This is the capital of the Lulua country. Natives had come from this village to Luebo a number of times asking for teachers. Haighs stayed at Kalamba several days. While there the natives begged them to stay and build a station. After their investigation tour of 450 miles through the Bampendi tribe, north to Djoka Punda 155 miles from Kalamba and then back to Luebo, Rev. Morrison, who had come to Luebo in 1896, recommended very strongly Kalamba as a site for a station.

Rev. Haigh sent his official report to the Congo Inland Mission Board suggesting that they begin their missionary work at Kalamba and use Djoka Punda as a transport station. The field was open, the natives demanded teachers and even the Catholic state official, Rev. J. O. Reavis, advised the natives that if they

wanted education they should get it from the Protestant missionaries and by his protection.  It was the op-
portune time to begin work there because civilization
was coming in with all of its evil influences and the
Catholics were beginning to send in priests. On the
other hand, the Presbyterians had more territory than
they could evangelize at the time and so all of these
reasons presented a real challenge to the Congo Inland
Mission Board. From this vantage point so near to Luebo, much help could be received from the Presbyterians. The missionaries have always appreciated this
help. Most of the mission work of Luebo was in the
Baluba-Lulua tribe.

On the other hand, Kalamba being on the western
border of the Baluba tribe was situated near enough
to other tribes that it might become an open door
to territory outside of that of the Baluba-Lulua. This
is proved by the records of the missionaries at the Kalamba station where in the report of 1940 Kalamba has
eleven tribes represented in their boys and girls at
the station. Most of these speak the language of the
Baluba people, Tshiluba.

Rev. and Mrs. Haigh made their second visit to
Kalamba in February, 1912. Here they remained until
the arrival of Rev. Stevenson. He arrived at Kalamba
May 11, 1912. He endorsed the decision of Rev. Haigh
that Kalamba was a good location for a mission station.
While Haighs were staying at Kalamba they were not
idly waiting but Mrs. Haigh began the first mission
work that was done in the Congo. A native Christian
teacher had been sent from Luebo who had started a
small school. Mrs. Haigh took over the work starting
with fifty pupils and in a week's time she had over a
hundred. Two hundred natives came out for Sunday
morning services including Chief Kalamba's sister. Before they left May 20, 1912, on an investigation tour,

they built a temporary hut, and temporary buildings for the meetings. The natives begged them to stay on permanently.

After a stay at Djoka Punda of three and a half months Rev. Haigh came to Kalamba and worked there from October 15 to December 15, 1912. He built a two-roomed house and established the first lighthouse in that territory. The plan was that Rev. and Mrs. Haigh should come to Kalamba in 1913 for permanent work while Rev. Stevenson would have charge of Djoka Punda with the new missionaries. This plan was, however, changed because of the death of Stevenson early in the year. The government gave an official grant for the territory at Kalamba, August, 1913. Rev. Haigh in writing to the home folks said that at Kalamba they would need two dwelling houses, boys' houses, store house and a church building. He emphasized the fact

Another station view in Congoland

that to the west of Kalamba was a large unoccupied field two hundred miles each way in the Bampendi tribe. Also to the south and west was the territory of the Batshoke people.

After the arrival of the first new missionaries at Djoka Punda, January 24, 1913 Rev. Haigh took Walter Scott Herr to Kalamba. Rev. Haigh returned from Kalamba April, 1913 and left Brother Herr alone. Herr became very sick and for four months the station was in the care of the Christian native Mutoto, whom Haigh had brought from Djoka Punda. In July, 1913 Janzens were sent to Kalamba to take charge of the work. In July, 1914 Miss Sarah Kroecker also went to Kalamba. Rev. Haigh, in one of his summary reports to the church papers, reports the following for Kalamba: the average attendance for Sunday preaching has been two hundred and eight and Sunday School two hundred and sixteen. School attendance is one hundred and twenty-six, eight hundred and twenty-five received medical treatment. Three outstations have been established. Two have native teachers and for the third, a teacher is sent from the station. In 1914 they built a permanent building valued at a thousand dollars. All of the supplies and mail that comes to Kalamba must come from Djoka Punda, 155 miles north. Goods have to be carried by native caravans.

As we come to the year 1916 in the history of Kalamba, a number of changes came about in the missionary personnel. Miss Sarah Kroecker left Kalamba and went to Djoka Punda where she married Dr. Oscar Anderson. When Rev. Haighs returned to the field in March, 1916, they brought with them Rev. and Mrs. J. P. Barkman. In the annual meeting held on the field it was decided that Barkmans should go to Kalamba. It is interesting to note here that not only are Barkmans among our oldest missionaries in terms of serv-

ice, but that they have served at the Kalamba station
from 1916 to the present time (1945). Their time is over
due now, (1945) for a furlough. It should be noted in
closing this part of the history of Kalamba in its pioneering stage that in these years permanent buildings
were established, outstations selected, a training
school started and the native church developed. Barkmans worked at Kalamba from 1916-1918 when they
had to come home because of Mrs. Barkman's health.
Rev. and Mrs. Janzen returned from their furlough
and took charge of the Kalamba station in 1919. Barkmans returned in 1920 and Janzens went to the new
station in the Bampendi tribe, Nyanga.

The Kalamba station made great progress in the
first fifteen years of its history. In a report sent to the
mission board for the year 1931 we have the interesting
information about the station and the church: the
number of acres in the concession to the Kalamba
station, 214; acres under cultivation for the missionaries, 4; for the natives, 43; value of the buildings,
permanent and temporary $4300; membership of the
church, 168; by the end of the year, 275; average church
attendance, 985; average Sunday School attendance,
572; men deacons, 2; assistant pastor, 1. In this report is
the following statement which is of interest: "Perhaps
the most encouraging event of the year is the progress
and growth of Kalamba station, where Brother Barkman has successfully organized a large school which
is claimed by the state authorities to be the best in the
Kasai district. A choir of boys and girls has been
trained to sing in parts and surpasses many choirs
at home both as to the quality of their voices and the
keeping in time. In the curriculum of the Kalamba
school was found besides the three R's, agriculture,
hygiene, physical geography, religion, music, nature
study, drawing, French and even lectures by a native

elder on practical problems of living.

In the pamphlet, "Twenty-five years of Mission Work in the Belgian Congo, a report for 1937 is sent by one of the missionaries. The report is as follows: The agricultural work of the station is carried on mostly by the boys and girls of the station. It is where they have an opportunity to learn practical lessons in farming, as well. Also providing food for themselves, not only as they have in the villages but a variety, such as meat, peanuts, beans, rice, millet, sweet potatoes, yams, etc. We have under cultivation about 67 acres and the Lord has blessed our efforts in a wonderful way.

The boys' Bible class opened with an enrollment of 25 pupils and the book of II Corinthians was the first subject of the new term. Many truths of vital importance to every Christian, and especially every Christian worker, were discussed. The boys asked some intelligent questions and we tried to answer them in the same way. We trust that those who were enrolled, although we are sorry to say that for various reasons, not all of them remained in the class until the close of the school term.

The girls' Bible classes had an enrollment of twelve pupils. There were eight pupils in one class and four in the other. The first group studied "The Gospel of John" and the second "Personal Work." The interest was good and the classes interesting. The second term the classes were united and all the pupils studied, "The Life of Christ." We trust that the Word of God will not return void but will accomplish that which the Lord pleases according to His promise in Isaiah 55:11.

The boys' school opened with an enrollment of 175 pupils, but the attendance kept dropping off be-

cause many of them were from the village and had to
stay out to attend their Circumcision Rites. This
brought the average attendance down to 114 for the
entire year, or school term.

The girls' school opened with an enrollment of 64
pupils and later on the attendance grew to 79, but drop-
ped again as girls, who came from the village, had to
help their mothers, and some of them were married.
Thus the average attendance was 66.

The Bible was stressed and given first place in the
curriculum and the pupils were reminded that "The
fear of the Lord is the beginning of knowledge." Many
Scripture passages were learned and many important
subjects were discussed with the pupils as regards
their relationship to God and their fellow men. The
interest was good and many things were learned that
will help the boys and girls in their future lives. We
feel that the possibilities are truly great. "How shall
they call on Him in whom they have not believed, and
how shall they believe in Him of whom they have not
heard? And how shall they hear without a preacher?"
Romans 10:14.

We truly praise the Lord again for those who are
willing to carry the gospel message to such who have
not heard, and others who have and do not understand
because they have not been born again. The gospel has
been preached and the Word expounded in the outstations as well as on the main stations again for another
year.

A goodly number have taken Christ as their Saviour and 107 were added to the church during the year.
But an interest for spiritual things seems to be a secondary thing for many, the material things, that they
count as wealth, come first. And it is much more so
since the Diamond Company is opening up many new

mines, and offering every inducement to those who received training in the mission. We are praying that the Lord will continue to work in our midst and we are looking to Him for a real revival among the Christians here as we are contemplating such meetings in the month of January.

The work in this department has been carried on as heretofore. We have experienced heartaches as well as joy in dealing with our girls. Some have become careless and strayed back into sin, while others are contented and happy, learning new songs and listening attentively to the gospel messages. Among this group a number have taken Christ as their Saviour. After all, His grace has been sufficient and His strength made perfect in weakness.

During this past year we admitted 31 new girls and ten were married while three left the compound, leaving 61 with us.

The industrial department has repaired a number of buildings, built one new one as well as finished the new dwelling here. Also several pieces of furniture were made.

We praise the Lord again for blessing the medical department so wonderfully this past year. Many have been cared for physically. And again many privileges were ours in upholding Christ among the suffering. The two native assistants have very ably cared for the work. They have cared for some that were very near beyond medical aid humanly speaking, but again every one left the ward well in body. There were no deaths on the station for which we are very grateful, realizing very keenly that the Lord saw fit in answering prayer, sparing lives for a purpose.

"Ho, every one that thirsteth, come ye to the waters, and he that hath no money; come ye, buy and eat;

yea, come, buy wine and milk without money and without price." Isaiah 55:1.

We have tried to stress personal work and that the love of God must show itself in deeds of kindness. Therefore we have had meetings one afternoon a week with the leaders' wives and a few others whom we felt we could sent out two by two, teaching and instructing them, thus helping them to become more efficient in doing personal work among their own people.

Our regular services are held on Thursday mornings and are well attended, despite the fact that there seems to be less interest for spiritual things.

As we look back over this past year our hearts are made to rejoice because the Lord has been with us in a wonderful way and has answered our many prayers. It is true the days have not all been sunshine and at times the battle raged; but the sun always shone behind the clouds and victory always came after the battle. We are encouraged to go forward into the new year and press the battle harder for He is on our side and we will not be defeated. We have a greater determination than ever to be our best for Him who gave His best for us.

One of the main sources for the writing of this history has been information received from the missionaries at home and on the field. This is particularly true of the chapters which give the history of the four stations. Rev. J. P. Barkman, who is one of our oldest missionaries, has furnished most of the material for the remaining part of this chapter. It will now be given in his own words.

Since we arrived here at Kalamba station just four years after Mr. and Mrs. Haigh arrived here for the first time we had the privilege of seeing the work in its infancy and to see it grow to its present size and proportions. The foundation had been laid and the work begun in its different departments. Mr. and Mrs. Janzen had just gone home on their first furlough.

The latter part of 1916 found six missionaries working on this station. Miss Anna Meester from Holland, Miss Elsa Lundberg and Mr. Henning Karlson from Sweden and Mr. Fredrick Johnson from England and Mr. and Mrs. J. P. Barkman from America.

We are grouping the work under the four heads as requested. In April, 1916, eleven young men were baptized who formed the nucleus of the Kalamba Church. Regular services were held on Sunday mornings and Sunday School in the afternoons. The Sunday School, composed of three classes, was now divided into five classes. The attendance at the Sunday morning service was rather small since many of the women took their hoes early in the morning and went to work in their fields but most of them returned in time for the Sunday School in the afternoon. There were also three services held during the week, Tuesday and Friday mornings at six o'clock and Wednesday night prayer meeting.

November, 1918 four more young men were baptized and added to the church. In 1920 the first three young women were baptized. Women's meetings were started in 1921 and later on, children's meetings and the young people's meeting were organized.

A Bible class was started at the beginning of the work for which later a two-years' course was arranged for those who wanted to go out as teachers. Afterwards this course was extended to three years. In the beginning only young men attended class but later on girls were also admitted. The first outstation teacher was sent into the Batshoke tribe as early as 1915.

In 1916 eight teachers were placed among the Bena
Mbuyi and the Batshoke tribes. These teachers, however, were out teaching only part time as they still
needed to attend school so they alternated three
months attending school and one month teaching and
preaching out in the villages until they had finished
the curriculum. In 1921 work was started in the Baku-
anfuya tribe, and in 1922 in the Bakete and the Kam-
bulu tribes. In 1929 the first teacher was sent into the
Badinga tribe who were still considered cannibals and
among whom it was not considered safe to travel. This
teacher was located in a village just on the border of
the tribe and later on other schools were opened farther into the tribe and in time they became more
friendly to the mission and consented to send their
children to the station school.

Since there were no government schools in this
district it was necessary for the mission to have a
school in order to teach the people to read the Word
of God. The attendance was not very large in the
beginning but good interest was manifested and by
1916 a few were already far enough advanced to read
the book of Bible lessons which had been translated
and printed by the American Presbyterian Congo
Mission. However, by far the largest part of the school
was still in the primary department and some of our
present leaders were still learning their A, B, C's. All
the classes of which there were four were taught
by the missionaries. The school now was organized
to make rapid strides in the way of education and we
soon had some pupils far enough along to assist the
missionaries who were only too glad to put some responsibility on the natives. This was an advantage in
several ways not only to the missionaries but also
to the natives. It was advantageous to the missionaries

in that it lightened the load of work which naturally rests upon them. Then it was advantageous to the natives in that it gave them a training in practical teaching before they were sent out as teachers to outstations. The idea in the native mind is that this is a white man's work and we are trying to impress upon them that it is their work, we are here to get it started and then help them to carry it on. If the time should ever come that all the white people should have to leave the responsibility would fall on them and God would then hold them responsible to carry on the work. As the work advanced the children finished school but some were too young to be sent out as teachers so in order to keep the children in school more grades were added to the course and more studies to the curricu-

Part of the harvest yielding fruit unto Eternal Life

lum. At first reading, writing and arithmetic were emphasized but later on to these were added geography, hygiene, language, agriculture, drawing and French. At the present time we are grading our school so as to conform to government regulations.

In the beginning the catechism class was conducted as a class by itself outside of school hours which was not as successful as it should have been, so later on it was inserted into the curriculum as a regular study divided up in the different classes and the children have to finish it as well as the other studies in order to pass into the next grade. In this way the children became more interested and they are now studying the different portions of God's Word, which helps to give them a fair idea of the plan of salvation. Our present enrollment in school is about three hundred.

Since all the school children came from heathen homes where they received no Christian training, a boarding school for boys was started right from the beginning. These boys living on the compound were required to work a certain number of hours daily for which they received their food and clothes, as well as their schooling. In 1916 about 25 or 30 boys were enrolled in the boarding school, some of them from this village and others from more distant villages who would have otherwise been too far away to attend school at the station. The missionaries soon came to the realization that in order to establish Christian homes and elevate family life more attention need to be paid to the girls. Very few girls were received in the school from the village at this time as they were kept at home to help their mothers in their fields. In 1919 a few girls were taken into the boarding school and by the end of 1920 there were 20 girls enrolled. Out of the group of twenty, thirteen became the wives of outstation teachers or of leaders, of deacons on the mission station. In school these girls kept up with the boys in their classes and year by year more boys and girls were enrolled in the boarding school, many coming from outside villages and from different tribes. They were under Christian influence and training for a number of years.

The native is musically inclined and so in 1920 a choir was organized of sixteen voices picked from the school children and teachers which proved to be a success from the beginning. To this nucleus others were added in time until it reached its highest number which was eighty. Four part singing was taught to which the natives took readily. In the beginning very simple songs were chosen to give them a good start and a good idea as to how things were to be done. Later on more difficult songs were chosen such as "Hallelujah for the Cross," in which the chorus goes in six parts, and others of similar type. This choir became a regular part of the Sunday morning service. After some time a male chorus was organized, of the young men and boys of this choir. Also a women's chorus was organized. These two organizations also proved a success and special music was furnished by at least one and sometimes two of these organizations in our Sunday morning and evening services. We often hear it said that it is easy to start something but to keep it going is quite another matter. It did not take us very long to realize this in the choir work, it has not always been easy. Some of the choir members finished their training and were sent out as teachers and the young men marrying girls also belonging to the choir which created empty spaces. Often those that left were some on whom the greatest burden of the choir rested. New ones had to be recruited who sometimes did not have as good voices as those that left which naturally lowered the quality a bit, other times the new recruits had better voices which improved the quality of the singing. Since music is included in the government regulations the choir naturally became part of their training. The boys and girls coming from outside villages seem to have good voices but not always true to pitch and special efforts had to be put forth to get them into line. These outside boys and girls brought with them the tribal jealousies which exist between the tribes sometimes to an overflowing measure and they had to be dealt with carefully. The boys from the different tribes ha dto stand side by side and sing as though it was a great pleasure when in fact it was a severe strain on their pride, but they had to obey orders. Choir training proved to be a fine thing to teach them obedience and unity. Training a choir is good training not only for the choir but also excellent training for the director. Perhaps the temper and the patience of the director receive the hardest punishment and this training of the temper and patience does not come amiss in the other phases of mission work. The natives are not very good leaders but they are very good followers which makes that part much easier for the director. In the beginning we used to have the organ to accompany the singing but later on it was used only at rehearsals. At present when we get all the four parts so that they can sing them well and we are ready to put them together. They always ask to "leave the organ and take the baton" they can follow that better because they can see it. The greatest thing of all that makes choir singing a success is the fact that we put special emphasis on singing to glorify God even as David of old says in his Psalm, "I will sing unto the Lord." Since we are doing that we have noted marked improvement in our singing. It is interesting as well as encouraging to hear the natives as they go about their work during the week, or while they are sitting around their camp fires in the evening sing these songs in perfect harmony.

"And Jesus went about all the cities and villages teaching in their synagogues and preaching the gospel of the Kingdom and healing all kinds of sickness and evrey disease among the people." Matthew 9:35. Along with teaching and preaching follows the care of the physical needs of the people. The mission station is surrounded by a population that is mainly dependent upon the missionaries for help in sickness. This population in order to receive adequate care requires the efforts of a trained medical staff. Unfortunately Kalamba station has had no doctor to take this responsibility and it has often been extremely difficult to diagnose and prescribe for the various ailments and diseases with which these people are afflicted. The nurses who have been at the station and have had to assume this work have keenly felt the responsibilty that was placed upon them in trying to do this difficult work without adequate training. No matter how good a training a nurse may have she is still not a doctor and should not be expected to do the work of such.

The first dispensary in 1916 was merely a box with a few simple medicines. As the naitves came with their diseases and bruised bodies the cure had to be found in the few simple remedies the missionaries had. In 1917 this box was deposited in a small mud hut especcially made for it. Here the medicines could be placed on a shelf and the rain could not interfere with treating the people. During 1919 a small two-roomed brick dispensary was built with a wide veranda which had been used for that purpose to the present time. From time to time new medicines were added to the limited

supply.  The natives have lost some of their fear and
superstition and more and more of them come to be
healed and some are willing to assist us in our care
for the sick.  God has often done to us the seemingly
impossible and we thank Him for it.  Many have
through the work in this department been brought into
contact with the mission and heard the gospel of Jesus Christ and learned to know Him as the great Physician of the body as well as the soul.

Another department that has made a large contribution to the work of the mission is the industrial.
Buildings continually need to be erected to be used
for homes, school houses and churches.  The first buildings were made of mud and sticks.  These are very
temporary because they become the food for white
ants.  In 1916 and 1917 a missionary building was made
of brick and a church building was made.  The church
building burned down in 1921 and has been replaced by
a building 112 feet long and 60 feet wide.  The last
building project at the station was a school unit begun
in 1939 and completed in 1941.  These are built of
granite stone instead of brick and have an iron roof.
After 1931 Mr. Sutton had charge of the industrial department.

The last  statistical report for 1944 is as follows:
number of missionaries, 4; native helpers, 3; assistant
pastor, 1; deacons, 2; number of church members, 1133;
converts awaiting baptism, 290; outstation teachers,
47; Sunday School attendance, 346; church, 375; prayer meeting, 210; Christian Endeavor, 215; Bible training
class, 31; boys, 31; girls, 6. Boys at station, 72; girls, 35;
regional schools, 1; rural schools, 47; teachers regional
school, 4; rural school, 47; station school, 16; school
attendance at station, 200; regional school, 66; rural
school, 1638. In the medical department, medical help-

ers, 3; dispensary patients, 514; patients treated, 703; microscopic examinations, 562. Number of acres cultivated, 65.

One of the problems for the mission board and the missionaries at Kalamba is the present location of the station as far as the future of the work is concerned. As stated before this station is on the western border of the Baluba tribe. Quite a large number of outstations are in the surrounding tribes but it is difficult to get the children from the outstations to the mission because of the hostile attitude of Kalamba village. Some feel that this should be made an itinerating station and the mission be moved farther west nearer the center of the field.

Just a word needs to be said concerning the attempt to establish a station in the Batshoke tribe. In 1930 under the leadership of Mr. Sutton the Holesa station was started. But because of opposition from the Diamond Company working in that territory it became necessary to give up the station. The work, however, continues under the native leader, Mundeke. The Christians at this place have six outstations which they support. Kalamba station has the oversight of this work.

One of the outstanding Christian natives at the Kalamba station was a young man named Kleinboy. He was brought by the Diamond Company from Angola to Tshikapa to be a foreman. Leaving that work about 1924 he came to Kalamba where he went to school and on confession of faith was baptized. After completing the course he went back to Angola, started mission work there and brought his converts to Kalamba to be baptized. He later left the place and went farther south, but the work went on under other leadership. Today there are 221 church members and six outstations. The work is self supporting.

The following missionaries have served at the Kalamba station: Janzens 1913-1921, Sarah Kroecker 1912-1915, Fredrick Johnson 1915-1916, Elsie Lundberg 1915-1918, Henning Karlson 1915-1918, Anna Meester 1915-1918, Barkmans 1916-1945, Suttons 1937-1942, Beckers 1923-1935, Miss Fannie Schmallenberger 1935-1945, Miss Mabel Sauder 1938-1945, Geo. B. Neufeld 1945.

### CHAPTER XIII

# Nyanga Station

As has been formerly stated a number of times, the Congo Inland Mission Board is responsible for the evangelization of the territory occupied by four large tribes with a number of smaller tribes. This territory, larger than the state of Illinois, has nearly four hundred thousand natives. The first two mission stations described in the former chapters are located in the Baluba-Lulua tribe, who have as their language, the Tshiluba. This is the official language of a number of the smaller tribes. It might be noted here that there are 523 languages and 320 dialects among the Bangu tribes. As we now come to the third station we find ourselves in the second large tribe called the Bampendi, whose native language is the Kipendi. There are no mission stations in the Bashilele and the Batshoke tribes. In 1930 an attempt was made to establish a station at Holesa but it became necessary to discontinue it. There is, however, work being done continually in these two tribes. Outstations are established by Charlesville in the Bashilele and by Kalamba in the Batshoke.

From the very beginning of our mission work in the Congo the missionaries were interested in establishing stations in the Bampendi tribe. In 1912, when Haighs and Rev. Stevenson made their investigation tour from Kalamba to Djoka Punda, they went through the Bampendi tribe and visited a number of villages. Rev. Haigh, in a personal letter states that on several occasions from 1912-1919 he visited among the Bampendi people and made investigations in view of open-

ing a new station.  The Congo Inland Mission Board
decided in its 1918 meeting to open a third and fourth
station, these two to be in the Bampendi tribe. In September, 1919 he with Rev. Sommer and Rev. Janzen
went to Nyange's village and met a governmental official for the purpose of selecting land for a mission
station.  While Janzens were at Kalamba they went to
Nyanga village and with the help of Sutton opened
the station in December, 1920.  Before this time, however, native Christian teachers from Kalamba had
been placed in certain strategic villages to bring the
natives the gospel and to prepare the way for the coming of the missionaries.  Teachers from the Baluba-
Lulua tribe helped in the Nyanga and Mukedi territory
till the Annual Conference of 1929 when it was decided that these teachers could go back to their own tribes.
Some of the teachers had asked for this permission.
In 1926 two young Bampendi men were sent out as
teachers in the outstations.  In 1936 Nyanga had thirty-nine outstations and a church membership of two
hundred and thirty.  In June, 1922 Janzens, who started the work at Nyanga, resigned from the Congo Inland Mission work and went to another field under
another board.  The Nyanga station was left in the
hands of a native teacher, Makesudi, until 1923.

From 1920, time of the opening of Nyanga station,
until 1923 a number of events took place in the home
field which affected the work in the Bampendi tribe.
Miss Alma Doering came back from Europe in 1919
and did considerable deputation work throughout the
churches under the Congo Inland Mission Board. She
was particularly interested in opening up the Bampendi work and establishing a number of stations. She
raised money specifically for this purpose. The North
Danvers Mennonite Church of the Central Conference

pledged $10,000 to this work in 1921. This was to be paid in five years. In 1921 the Congo Inland Mission Board was enlarged by the joining of Grand Rapids Auxiliary. This Auxiliary was particularly interested in the sending of missionaries and money for the Bampendi work. The year 1923 is an outstanding year in the fact that the largest number of missionaries ever sent to the field in one year were sent this year. Some of these came from the Grand Rapids Auxiliary. Mr. and Mrs. Raphael Valentine, supported by the Grand Rapids Auxiliary, came out in 1923 and took charge of the work at Nyanga. Later in the same year, November, 1923 Miss Clio Briggs and Miss Beulah MacMillen also came to the Nyanga station. Miss Agnes Sprunger came from Mukedi and helped out at Nyanga until the coming of Miss Kornelia Unrau in June, 1926. The other named missionaries left in 1926. January 17, 1927, Rev. and Mrs. Frank J. Enns came to take charge of the station at Nyanga and they are at present serving at this station. The following report con-

One of the first "churches" in our mission work

cerning the work at Nyanga was kindly furnished by
Rev. and Mrs. Enns and Miss Unrau.

The work at the station, though still in its beginnings, was encouraging. There were a goodly number
of girls and boys in the girls' and boys' homes. A mission village for married people had been started. There
was a school, chapel exercises were held, also Sunday
morning and evening services, and prayer meetings.
The church had only about ten members, but quite a
few of the children had made a decision to follow
Christ. Two young Bampendi men had been made
leaders at the station. Work in distant outstations was
done by four teachers who had come from the Charlesville district. Eight near-by villages were served by
school boys from the station. Medical aid was given
from a small dispensary. The necessary buildings had
been erected from temporary material, two of which
are still standing. One is the old chapel built by Miss
Briggs in 1926, the other is an old two-room mud house
first built by Mr. Janzen and later partly rebuilt by
Miss Briggs. It has served as a dwelling house, store
house, again as dwelling house, and is now serving
as a schoolhouse.

Looking over the work of the station the last ten
years we find much reason to praise God. In an early
report of 1924 we find the beginning of this mission
work in this new station. At Nyanga, number of boys
in training, 15. A recent letter from Misses MacMillen
and Briggs shows sixteen boys and eight girls in training. To get the girls in a new tribe is the task of a
genius. Most of the girls are married when they are
very small; number in Sunday School 36; teachers 2;
baptized Christians 4; and teachers in outstations 6.
The work done by these native missionaries has been
on the whole effective and far reaching. We might

make special mention of Kamba and Badiasa who were especially successful in winning boys for Christ and inspiring them to Christian service while there, and of Makasudi who has given long service and is still in the work of the Lord. He had been one of the early converts at Charlesville and received his early schooling while a workman there.

At the end of our last statistical year, 1935, church membership stood at 239. The number of outstations had grown to thirty-nine. The medical work has grown. A new dispensary is being erected of stone. Besides the work at the dispensary on the station we now have two medical boys treating sores in distant villages. Where at the station school only a few of the grades were taught a five year course is now given. The last statistics show an average attendance of 133, but present enrollment is considerably higher. Teacher-evangelists are being trained in Bible training classes. Sunday School is a regular part of the Sunday worship at the station and at most outstations. Good interest is manifested in our Christian Endeavor that was started five years ago. A trained choir sings at the Sunday morning service.

Since we found building stone in the vicinity of our station four years ago a good beginning in the building of more permanent buildings has been made. Combined with sun-dried bricks for the inside, five buildings have been built with this hard stone, a guest house, a dwelling house, a garage, a carpenter shop, and a kitchen-store house for the girls' home. A large cistern has also been built with this stone. Thus the prayer of many at our station for building material has been answered.

The rest of Rev. Enns' report for 1935 is in the form of important events.

December 17, 1926—Lightning strikes a house on the mission village. Two Christian boys are instantly killed, and one is burned severely.

February, 1929—A teachers' Bible Training Class is started.

September, 1929—We place first group of Bampendi student-teachers in distant outstations.

March 7, 1930—First Nyanga car arrives, a Ford Model A. touring car.

November 17, 1930 — The newest feature of the work at Nyanga is the Kindergarten. It would be more truthful to divide it and call part of it a "cradle roll," for some of the children are only two years old. There are about twenty little ones, sons and daughters of the Christians who are in school here.

September, 1931—Revival meetings are held with Mr. Moser as speaker. Chief Kakotshi and Sub-chief Kinzongo accept Christ. Kinzongo burns his witchcraft in the center of the village.

January 10, 1932—We have our first C. E. Program.

April, 1932—First groups of day school pupils and Teachers' Bible Training class finish their respective courses.

November 4, 1932 — Saturday night at eleven o'clock, October the 29th, Kinzongo passed quietly away. It was not the passing away of just another native. Besides being a sub-chief in Kunyi's village he was a Christian—not just an ordinary Christian who had accepted Christ with the crowd, not one who had been in school and daily listened to the gospel stories —rent out of dark heathenism he was transplanted into the kingdom of Light. It is only a little more than a year ago that he accepted Christ. Aroused by the sudden death of a young man, I am told he, began to think seriously about his soul. A revival meeting at the mission and personal work brought him to where

he accepted Christ. Again and again we had been told
by the older people of this territory that the Mbimbi ya
Nzambi (Word of God) is for children and not for the
older people who have grown up in spirit worship and
the customs of the tribe. But Kinzongo was a big man
in the affairs of the tribe, a medicine man, a blacksmith,
and a hunter, an older man of about fifty years, a man
with several wives and a father of around thirty children.  All this worked against him. But the call came
to him like it did to Paul long ago, and he counted it
all but loss that he might win Christ.  As Malenka,
the headman of the village put it at the funeral Monday when reviewing the affairs of the one who had
passed away. He said that when Kinzongo accepted
Christ he had been told the Word of God is only for
children, but Kinzongo insisted that it was AN AF-
FAIR OF HIS HEART.  And truly all along the way of
his short Christian life he has borne out that testimony
that it was an affair of the heart.

March, 1935—The hunger in many villages is so
great because of the damage the locusts did that people
dig up roots in the forests and eat them. At Tshingila
two people died because they ate a poisonous tuber.

September 25, 1936 — Our evangelistic work has
caused us much concern, and many prayers have gone
up. The testing time has come, and many who confessed were not willing to surrender all—they just lost
out.

October 7, 1936—On Sunday evening, September
27, at our regular Sunday evening service part of the
evening was  spent in prayer for our two spiritual leaders, who were about to start an evangelistic trip to the
outstation villages which would last for about two
weeks. The purpose was to visit the Christians and to
encourage and strengthen them in their life and work
of love and faith.  I was impressed how the Christians

here at the mission prayed so earnestly for God's guid-
ances, blessing and protection upon their leaders. Ex-
actly a week later on Sunday evening of October 4, it
pleased the Lord to call home our dear deacon, Kit-
amba, or Daniel.  While at his work in a village he
was struck by lightning and entered eternity instantly.

October 11-13, 1936—The first inspirational conference of Christian women of Nyanga territory is held.
"Bless the Lord, O my soul, and forget not all his  bene-
fits."

During this period represented by this report, the
question came up seriously concerning the merging
of the Nyanga work with Mukedi.  The Field Committee took such action in July, 1930. The Annual Conference in December, 1930 supported the decision of
the Field Committee.  The reason for it seemed to be
that Nyanga had a sparse population of only 18,000
against 100,000 in the Mukedi field. The Congo Inland
Mission Board, however, discouraged the merger and
Nyanga continued as an independent station. This brief
report of 1931 would rather justify the position of the
board. Acres under cultivation by the missionaries, 2;
by the natives, 40; membership January 1, 1932, 52;
catechumens, 134; average church attendance, 700;
average Sunday School attendance, 225; ordained men
deacons, 2.

The missionaries' report from the field has reports
on the regular departments of evangelistic, educational,
medical and industrial.  The first one is evangelistic.
At the beginning of 1929 the Bible Training Class to
prepare teacher-evangelists for their work was started.  The enrollment at the close of the first year was
twenty-five.  This  training  school  was  continued
through the years, and has become one of the most important works on the station.  It has made possible
the expansion of the work so that instead of the fifteen

outstations we had when this class began we now have
fifty-four, and three regional schools. In its early years
the training class had but one teacher, a missionary,
but gradually others began to help, so that today three
missionaries and two native workers teach one or more
class periods. A three years course is offered. The training class has at present thirty-five students, six of
whom are girls and women.

The year 1929 is also important in that in that year
the number of our outstations was more than doubled.
This came about in this wise. During the vacation
month of August we sent Bible Training Class boys out
two by two in the different directions to make a survey
of the territory, to find the places of the villages and
count the houses so we could make an estimate of the
population. The boys also testified for Christ as opportunities presented themselves.

When the boys returned with the information we
sought for, they reported indifference and even opposition in more distant villages, and gross ignorance
of the work we are trying to do. We felt that to en-
lighten the people they needed contact with the mission and mission people, and that the time to act had
come. Any delay might make it harder for us later. To
sent teachers out to stay permanently was out of the
question, as the training of the boys could not be in-
terfered with. There was one way open, to extend our
system of having the boys teach part time. They had
some experience from teaching in near-by villages.
Others might take their places and they go to distant
villages. In 1927, before we had our Bible Training
Class, we had started schools in two villages about
thirteen miles away with students as teachers. They
were out for one week and in for their studies the other week, and it worked.

We now decided to teach Bible Training Class

rather intensively one week, while for the other week the boys were to be sent out to teach in the distant villages. The plan was accepted enthusiastically by the boys. A missionary and the native deacon accordingly made an itinerary to place boys in strategic villages. At many of the places the teachers were accepted with enthusiasm. The demand was greater than the supply. In most instances this arrangement has proved a great blessing. It gave a great impetus to the work, and the boys gained much experience while still in training. While this arrangement of having a Bible Training Class only every other week has disadvantages we have continued it till the present. Our supply of teachers who have finished the Training Class seems never to be enough to meet the demand so that some have to go out while in training.

In 1940 a section of our Nyanga territory that had seemingly been closed to Protestant work before opened to us. It is the section between the Luovo River and Tshikapa. Some boys from there came to our station in May to go to school. One of them said that their chief wanted one of our teachers. After we had placed a teacher-evangelist in that village it did not take two months till we had found opportunity to place four more in that section.

The following figures reveal the expansion of the outstation work. In 1926, 11 outstation schools; 1927, 13; 1929, 33; 1933, 35; 1940, 54. Three regional schools have been established where school work is given above second grade. Practically all of the itinerating work is done in relation to the outstation schools. The missionary visits these schools about twice a year. Special services are held which are an encouragement to the teachers but are evangelistic in nature. In 1934, 1319 expressed a desire to accept Christ but when the testing time comes some go back to their heathen customs.

The Sunday School was started in 1928. In 1940 there were sixteen classes. The men and women meet separately. The lesson helps have been prepared for both Nyanga and Mukedi. The Christian Endeavor meetings began January 10, 1932. Children gather to learn songs, Bible verses and also give public programs. A personal workers group was organized in 1936 where native Christians are trained to win others for Christ.

**The new church at Nyanga**

In the industrial work at the Nyanga station the outstanding things are the cistern and the new church. The cistern is of stone and has a capacity of 11,500 gallons, and proves very useful. With the completion of this cistern much of our water problem was solved. We are about a mile from the river. This cistern supplies all the missionary dwellings and the industrial work with water for about nine months in the year. The church is built in the shape of a cross, and will seat about 800 people. A thousand people or more can be crowded into it when necessary. The church has arches all along the sides, and a tower and bell in front above the entrance. The church is furnished with heavy benches having back rests—all native labor —from the felling of trees to the planning and nailing of the benches. Most of these benches have also been paid for by the natives.

The school began in 1921. In 1923 a class of fifteen boys was taught for two terms of three months each. By 1926 the school term was nine months and the enrollment went up to one hundred. When the standard of the school was raised, interest and enthusiasm on the part of the pupils rose also. In 1928 the first course of study was worked out and typed. It gave the outline for teaching Bible stories, Scripture memory work, reading, writing, and number work. In April, 1932 the first class of twenty-one boys graduated from the course. At this time Protestant missions in Congo were beginning to try to bring their schools up to state standard, and to conform to state program. Thus in the beginning of 1935 a thirty-five page course of study was arranged and printed on the multigraph. This course follows as nearly as possible the Kimpese Course of Study prepared by the missions of the Lower Congo which meets government regulations. Our course after five years use needs revision.

Before a pupil enters the first year he does pre-standard work. The first two years of graded work comprise the first degree, and the last three years, the second degree school. So it takes a pupil six years to finish the course. The government puts no restriction on teaching religion. We see here our golden opportunity to teach the Life-giving Word. The subjects stressed most are religion, reading, writing, and arithmetic, with due emphasis on hygiene, agriculture, geography, rudiments of music, conduct lessons, general knowledge, handicraft, and supervised play.

Under religion we have: 1.—Classes in Scripture

memory work, each class learning between thirty and sixty Bible verses a semester. 2.—Catechism taught from beginners' class to and including fourth year. 3.— Bible stories in all grades. 4.—Music, ten minutes daily of general singing, sacred songs only, and notation in the last grade. As reading texts we use three readers and then the New Testament and the Bible. Every pupil in the third grade is required to own his own Bible. Conduct lessons are based on Bible stories. Practical problems in arithmetic connect up with the daily life of Christians.

The boys, girls, and workmen living on the mission compound still make up the greater part of our station school. The number from near-by villages is increasing every semester, and applications from far away villages also keep coming in. We can accept only some, so unless they are from a corner where there is no out-station teacher, they must be able to read the New Testament before they can enter the station school. Our largest enrollment is 297.

Since our work was the first in this tribe there were no text books. In 1923 two readers were translated into the Kimpende from the Tshiluba language. In 1928 a sixty page primer-reader was compiled and multi-graphed here. In 1935 a revised second edition was printed at Charlesville, and in 1940 a third. In 1930 and 1931 two books, one on hygiene and one on geography were prepared. In 1938 a language for the second and third grade was translated and in 1939 a Bible memory verse booklet was revised. For other text books in the lower grades we are indebted to Jukedi, and for the upper grades to the American Presbyterian Mission.

Handicraft has been stressed for a number of years. Each pupil, the semester before graduation must present a number of satisfactory articles of handicraft that he has chosen as **his** craft, and has learned to make. This is to help them to earn extra money to make their living, and also that valuable native craft shall not be lost. They make baskets of different kinds, knives from iron, mats, raffia cloth woven on hand looms, flour sieves, salt strainers, suitcases, wooden spoons, forks, and dippers.

A medical ward, a place of physical healing and an open door to give the Gospel story

The medical work here at Nyanga began on a very small scale in 1926. At first we gave out medicines from the veranda of our house, but when people began to come from villages we had to find a different place. In July the same year a small chicken house was prepared as a dispensary and the patients were treated there. In August, 1926, the same year people with large ulcers were brought to us. They began to gain confidence in our medicines. In October we had up to twenty patients a day, and in December thirty patients. It was a great joy that we could relieve suffering. One of the touching experiences in medical work is the many painful open sores of the natives. Another is their care of the babies. Many babies die because of exposure, lack of proper food and care. In October, 1926 the first baby with pneumonia was trusted to our care. The Lord heard our prayers and the baby responded to our care to the great joy of the parents. In December, 1926 the first Mupendi baby was born on the station. This helped to break down the heathen customs and use of fetishes.

The call of the sick is continuous. Day and night they come with their diseases or bruises. The lack of sanitary conditions aids in the spreading of diseases so the medical missionary not only cures the patient but also teaches people the conditions of health and sanitation. In 1929 a dispensary was built, with a large veranda so that ulcer cases could be treated there. As high as seventy patients come in one day. Another interesting part of the medical work is the training of promising young men in medicine. In 1930 a young man was sent to Luebo and completed a three year course. Other young men were selected from time to time and are in training for work not only on the station but also on the outstations.

Another work on the station is that of the girls. This started in 1925. These girls came from various sources. Some came because of sickness and after they received help they stayed with the station. Some came because they were orphans and wanted a home. A few also came from some of the chiefs after the missionaries had pled for them. By 1929 the station had fortyeight girls. By this time some of the girls come to the station voluntarily while some are sent there by their prospective husbands. After these girls are trained and become Christians they become the wives of the native Christian young men. By 1940 the station had over sixty girls.

The natives enjoy singing and love to hear others

sing. In many types of work the native seems to reach his limit or capacity quicker than in music. The natives do not mind the drill work which is very necessary for good singing.

Some missionaries think that one should use the native melodies and put sacred words to them. Others think that the native melodies have evil association connected with them, and therefore should not be used. Some argue that our songs which are based on the chromatic scale do not come natural with the natives. 'Tis true that their melodies are in the minor key and are based on a simpler scale. However, with sufficient drill and practice the natives sing our gospel hymns with remarkable ease and accuracy. Of course, they cannot play them on their native instruments, but some of their instruments are too crude for the more intelligent natives.

The natives take quite readily to conducting or beating time. At our station Mr. Enns has been teaching conducting as a course in the day school. Thus by the time some of our natives finish the Bible School, they are pretty good conductors for our mixed choir. We use mostly four part harmony. It appeals to the natives.

The following report for the close of 1944 shows the progress of the work at Nyanga: number of missionaries 4; native helpers 4; assistant pastors 1; number of church members 445; converts awaiting baptism 298; Sunday School attendance 633; church service 586; prayer meeting attendance 365; Christian Endeavor 210; number of pupils enrolled in Bible Training Class 75; native pupils at the station 83; number of regional schools 5; rural schools 70; number of teachers in regional schools 14; number of teachers in rural schools 70; primary school attendance at the station 320; attendance at the regional schools 158; rural schools 2301. In the medical department there are five native helpers. The medical patients for 1944 were 11-62; number of patients treated 1239; microscopic examinations made 490. The number of acres cultivated thirty-two.

The following missionaries have served at the Nyanga station during the time 1920-1945; Janzens 1920-1922, Miss Agnes Sprunger 1925, Mr. and Mrs. Valentine 1923-1925, Miss Briggs and Miss MacMillen 1923-1927, Mr. and Mrs. Milton Amie 1928-1932, Rev. and Mrs. Frank J. Enns 1927-1945, Miss Kornelia Unrau 1926-1945, Rev. and Mrs. Henry Toews 1936-1943, Miss Anna H. Quiring 1936-1943, Miss Erma Birky 19-30-1931, Dr. Rudolph Unruh 1934.

### CHAPTER XIV

# Mukedi Station

The fourth station in the Congo Inland Mission territory and the second in the Bampendi tribe is about seventy miles west of Nyanga. At the time mentioned in the history of Nyanga station when the Grand Rapids Auxiliary became a part of our mission board, efforts were made to establish a number of stations in the Bampendi tribe. It had been the desire of the Congo Inland Mission Board since the beginning of our mission work to open up mission work in all our tribes. Rev. Haigh stated in a personal letter that in his investigations among the Bampendi people he had gone as far as the Mukedi village. The Congo Inland Mission Board decided in its 1918 meeting to open a third and fourth station in the Bampendi tribe.

After the opening of Nyanga the missionaries went west to investigate a suitable location for another station. This was in 1921. The mission board at home had given official sanction in 1921 to the opening of a new station near Mukedi village. A native teacher-evangelist had been placed at Mukedi when the site was chosen in 1921.

October 13, 1923 Rev. Lester Bixel, (deceased) Rev. and Mrs. H. H. Moser and Miss Erma Birkey arrived at Mukedi. Mosers and Miss Birkey had come to the field in the early part of 1923. They camped in the village three months while a temporary shelter was being built. December 13, 1923 they moved into the bamboo house with a grass roof, in the site that had been chosen for them. There was no building near, therefore this very temporary house. After Christmas Mr. Bixel went back to Charlesville. He was stationed there and was

"In days gone by"

kindly loaned to us to help build the first house.

Though they were told not to try to do much station work, but to apply themselves to learning the unwritten language of this tribe, the Kipende, they started a school with about ten boys who wanted to attend. They had no school house, so had it in the morning under a shade tree. They did a little medical work too. There was no government doctor nor any medical aid until a while after they had been there.

The 30th day of April Miss Alma Doering and Miss Agnes Sprunger came to us, Miss Sprunger had been at Nyanga a few months, and had started translating in Kipende. Some of the difficulties which the missionaries faced in the beginning of their work were first to get workmen to do their building and second to get food. Often they could not even buy an egg and felt fortunate when they could get a chicken.

In the first year's stay at Mukedi the missionaries met with a great tragedy. It seemed that this new station was much more subject to lightning than the other stations. Rev. Moser said that in five weeks time lightning struck twice not over seventy yards away from the house. On May 20, 1924 lightning struck the home of Rev. and Mrs. Moser and destroyed the building and all its contents. The site had been very undesirable and so the missionaries decided to select another site. Rev. and Mrs. O. L. Sutton came from Charlesville June 25, 1924 to help them select another site. Rev. Sutton was the industrial man on the field. The present site, only about two miles from the first one, was selected and as soon as the state official gave us workmen the building began. Three months later they moved into the first house on the new site, and finished it after they were living in it. Much clearing had to be done after they moved. The new site is a beautiful place, and there is stone for building on hill

sides very near.  There are good springs, and it is
about 2700 feet above sea level. The soil is by no means
good, but palm trees thrive and there are other trees
on the place. The other site was a bleak lonely place.
They were the laughing stalk of the whole district.
The location was then changed to a site nearer to the
village.  A missionary from the Methodist Mission in
traveling through the Congo on his way to the West
Africa Conference visited at Mukedi a short time. He
said that he believed it was the most beautiful station
in its surroundings in the Congo. The first missionaries
there, Mosers, Miss Erma Birkey and Miss Sprunger
are still working at that station. The report of their
work with others has been kindly written by the missionaries.

The difficulties encountered by the early missionaries and the progress finally made is told in an interesting manner by Miss Erma Birkey.  The first Christmas we were at Mukedi we wanted to have a meeting
for the natives. We also went to Nzaji that day.  We
sang several songs in Kipende, then closed our eyes to
pray. When we opened our eyes, we found that our
audience had fled.  We learned afterward that they
thought they would get sleeping sickness if they would
close their eyes to pray.  On Sunday mornings a few
little boys who were in the teacher's school, would
come to the meeting.

The people in the villages took no notice of the
dedication of the first chapel in 1924. We invited them
to come too. Those first years we could not have children's meetings. They were so afraid of us that they
would scamper away when we called them. We were
living in Mukedi village two weeks when we saw the
first women and girls. One day we were plastering our
earthen oven with clay; when they saw white women
with mud on their hands they came out of hiding.

The first years we were here the people wanted medicine to rub on their heads, or where ever they had a pain. They would not risk drinking medicine we gave them. Sometimes we told them they must drink salts, they spilled most of it, but when we put a price on it, they drank every drop. Now they are willing to pay for medical treatment. Mothers with twins come to the hospital right after the babies are born to get away from the taboos for twins in the village, and to get the care they get here.

When we wanted to start a boarding school no one wanted to come. We asked the chiefs for some boys. One of the missionaries was very much surprised when he heard, after he had gone home to America, that there were girls in the boarding school at Mukedi. The first girl who was given us by the chief, Kalongonia of Mukedi, cried when she came. She did not

"A typical School Building for our beginnings in the Congo"

want to eat or work nor do anything. The second one took a very different attitude; she seemed to want to make the most of her new way of living. Now we do not ask for girls or boys to come to the mission. Boys, especially must learn to read in the village schools, then they may come to the mission school, or to the regional school. Those from the near-by villages live at home and come to school. Many of the first boys came to the mission for the clothes and salt rations we gave them. They did not realize that there was work and school in the bargain. Now they are willing to come to school from the villages and pay their tuition for second degree school. We gave all the pupils their books and slates in the beginning of the school at Mukedi. Now they buy most of their school supplies.

There has been a favorable change in the attitude of the people toward us in eighteen years. We can get all the workmen we want. The people come with food to our doors and are glad for salt in exchange.

When we dedicated the large chapel August 11, 1940 there were more than two thousand people crowded into the building. The Christmas service in 1939 attracted more than two thousand people. There were three thousand people at the baptismal service in November, 1939. Children's meetings on Sunday mornings range from two hundred to over a thousand. The average attendance at the Sunday morning services for this year has been over a thousand. Now we have thirty-five teacher-evangelists in the district. The gospel is being given in the villages every Saturday morning by the Bible students. A report given in 1931 will reveal the progress made at Mukedi from 1923 to 1931. Acres under cultivation for missionaries 4; for natives 60; church membership 64; catechumens 68; average church attendance 217; average attendance at Sunday School 217. This report continues by the missionaries in the pamphlet, "Twenty-five Years of Mission Work in the Congo." One who has not been at Mukedi since 1930 on Sunday would notice bigger crowds coming to the morning and evening service. Though we should have an attendance of four thousand instead of four or five hundred. There are more than that many people within easy walking distance of the mission. The native drum does not attract as many to church as to the dance. On alternate Sunday mornings there is a native evangelist who gives the Word now; in former years only the missionaries did the preaching. There is a consciousness of sin among the Christians, which, until the last few years was lacking. There are those who show sorrow and repentance for hidden sin. "The entrance of thy word giveth light." The Sunday evening services and the daily morning chapel services are entirely in charge of the native Christians. What an encouragement these spiritual children are to us. We have been very much encouraged in recent years to know that many of these children look to some of the older native Christians as their spiritual parents.

The evangelistic field is large and we could put out many more teacher-evangelists. The villages in this district want a teacher, but they want only a very few children to attend school. In this tribe the children belong to the mother's family, and they do not want to leave the old customs. They prefer not to have their children know how to read. The district has opened wonderfully during the last eight years. Before 1930 there were not so many calls for teacher-evangelists, and the people seemed to think that the mission standard was too high. Now they seem to see that a high standard is ideal, but most of them prefer to live on a lower plane. Only those who are saved try to attain a Christian standard.

The school on the mission station at Mukedi is fed

by the village schools. We try not to take students from villages where we have teachers, who have not attained a certain standard in the village school. That way we have compartively few who cannot read when they start in the school on the mission station. In former years we had more beginners' classes than advanced, and the school on the station was smaller than now.

Since 1930 the Bible classes have increased so that we have three classes instead of one. There are now fifty-four students in the Bible classes. These are preparatory classes for the teacher-evangelists in the villages. On Saturday mornings these Bible students go out to the villages for evangelistic services. They go to villages where we have no teachers. They come home with varied reports. Some have big attentive audiences, others are laughed at, and in some villages it is sometimes hard to get an audience. Most of the villages to which these groups go on Saturday are not within easy walking distance from the mission.

The girls' work has made as big a change in the last eight years as any department. Formerly we had to ask the chiefs for girls for the mission boarding school. They sent us slaves and the undesirables in many cases. They were a very few who chose to come. Now we have more than we can take care of, and they come by their on choice, or from the village schools. There are nine girls in the Bible classes. The lives of some of the Christian women, who have had severe tests, demonstrate the saving power of God in their hearts. These Christian women were some of the first girls in the mission boarding school.

There have also been some encouraging advances in the boys' work. The boys formerly came from the villages without a knowledge of Christian customs or of letters. Now they come, for the most part, from the schools in the district, and some of them have already accepted Christ as their Saviour. During their training on the mission they get Bible School and practical training in Christian work. The boys and men learn that it is just as honorable for a man to hoe in the field as for the women. They learn to build better houses than those in the villages. A Christian with a clean heart is not satisfied with dirty clothes; and they learn that it takes energy and strength to keep clean.

The parents of children learn that it is possible for the children to grow up without fetishes and charms. In fact the heathen people in the villages near the mission have observed that there are many more babies and little children in the Christian families than in the pagan families. Infant mortality is high in the pagan villages.

Necessity has made us train some of the natives certain trades. We need furniture and woodwork for the buildings, therefore we had to train carpenters.

Native helpers in the Medical work with "little prize packages"

We needed masons to build houses. We needed books for the school on the station and in the district schools.

Since this language was reduced to writing within the last fifteen years, we had to produce our own books. We trained native printers for that work. When the natives began to wear European clothes, we needed native tailors.

The stone for building was first experimented with in 1930. The third missionary dwelling is under construction at the moment. There is a stone hospital, and two wards for black patients. There is also a stone house used for white patients and for missionaries in transit. There are three stone dormitories and a kitchen for the native girls. There are various small houses, such as a gas house and garage, office, etc. There are fifteen houses with stone walls and tin roofs, and three stone houses with grass roofs. The tall stately palms, the ravine, and the beautiful scenery was here when we came. If you would have come to Mukedi before 1930, you would have found us living in mud houses with grass roofs. Our living quarters now are a pleasant contrast to eight years ago. We praise our Heavenly Father for all the good and beautiful things. Besides the buildings mentioned by Rev. Moser which were built in 1936 the following have been added, girls' camp, five stone buildings, started in 1936, finished in 1939; hospital ward for natives, 1937; missionary residence 1938; three school buildings with three rooms each completed in 1940; native leaders house with grass roof 1940. All of these buildings except two are made of stone. These buildings were all built with budget money and missionary gifts except three. Gifts were also made for the iron roofs of the hospital for white people and for the second and third missionary residence.

There is a phase of missionary work done at Mukedi which is rather unique. Just as Nazareth, the home of Jesus, was just a short distance from the world highway from the West to the Orient where Jesus met peoples of many nationalities, so Mukedi is just a short distance from a national highway. The description of it is given by Miss Birkey. It may be of interest to you to know that Mukedi is just a half mile from the highway from the west coast to the east coast. From Matadi to Luluaburg a railroad center. We very often have guests for the night. We are just a nice day's drive from Leverville or Kikwit to either Luebo or Tshikapa. That is we are just about half way between those centers. Being on the highway people who want a place for the night look out for us. It is not unusual to have people stop after dark, or even in the wee hours of the morning for a bed and gas. This is about the only place between those places where people can get gas. We have had quite a variety of guests. Missionaries, commercial people, government people, theatrical people, and tourists. It gives us a wonderful opportunity to give our testimony to these people. If we would name the number of nationalities we have entertained it too would make an interesting list.

The mission work at the Mukedi station consists of the activities on the station as well as that of establishing outstations. School on the station started November 25, 1924 with twenty-two boys. This was enlarged to a boarding school for boys and girls by 1926. These native young people were taught elementary courses as well as agricultural, medical and industrial work. All this training, however, with the one goal in mind of bringing these natives to a saving knowledge of Jesus Christ as their personal Saviour. The schedule of the day was, rising at 5:30; chapel 6:00-6:15 and then work from 6:15-11:30; from 1:30-5:30 P. M. everyone went to school except a few workmen. There are at present over seventy girls at the mission with varied ages. Some of these girls have accepted

Christ and will become wives of the teacher-evangelists.

The itinerating work of Mukedi station was at first
getting acquainted with the people, learning their customs and language. But by 1925 a few teachers were
establishing in the near-by villages. By 1940 there were
thirty-five teacher-evangelists. The first regional
school was begun in 1939. These schools neces-
sitated the establishment of a Bible School by 1926.
The school has had graduates each year since then.
The course has now been extended from two years to
three years. Another interesting phase of the outstation work is what is called the moonlight meetings.
These meetings are held three evenings a week in different villages. The attendance averages from two to
five hundred. The natives particularly enjoy the singing. The work at the mission the first ten years was
very difficult. There was opposition from the Catholics and through them brought opposition from the
native chiefs. But through the outstation work and the
moonlight meetings there came a great revival. In 19-
39 the Sunday morning church service increased from
five hundred in May to three thousand in November.
People came after the church service to say that they
had destroyed their idols and witchcraft and they
wanted to know the Lord. Some Sundays there were
four hundred confessions. Each one was dealt with
personally. A few did not understand what it was
all about, and just followed the crowd, but there were
those who had a clear testimony that made our hearts
rejoice. Quite a number of very old people have been
saved and died rejoicing instead of the heathen way,
with fear. There was great rejoicing in the village when
witch doctors confessed their work. (They are not supposed to be known in this tribe.) Murderers confessed
having killed a number of people, etc. Some of them

were afraid to tell what they had done and came like
Nicodemus. Those were days of very much rejoicing
at Mukedi as well as among the angels in heaven. Because of this increased attendance of the natives the
chapel was too small to accommodate all of them. Children met under the palm trees, the highest number
being eight hundred. In 1939 there were over two
thousand confessions. A new chapel was built and
dedicated August 11, 1940. It accommodates about two
thousand people. In 1927 the first group of converts
were baptized numbering seventeen. By 1940 there
were two hundred and twenty. 2530 were on the waiting list to be baptized.

One of the problems which faces the missionary
in our field is the language. The missionaries in the
Baluba-Lulua tribe were fortunate in the fact that this
problem had been practically solved by the Southern
Presbyterians from whom they could get their literature. The missionaries must always be grateful for the
splendid work of Dr. Morrison of the Luebo station.
But in the Nyanga and Mukedi stations it was different. They are in the Bampendi tribe and the language
here is entirely different from the Tshiluba. It is the
Kipendi language. The dialect of Nyanga is even different than the dialect of Mukedi. The one person who
has been largely responsible for translating the Bible
into the Kipendi language has been Miss Agnes Sprunger. She came to the field May 19, 1916 and is now in
her fifth term. She is one of our oldest missionaries in
service on the field. When the station at Nyanga was
opened Miss Sprunger came there in 1923 and began
with the translations in the Kipendi language. She was
aided by a native teacher, Kamba James, who had
been in a Bampendi village several years. Miss Sprunger used the English and the Tshiluba Bible. During
the years she was at Nyanga she translated about half

of the English Tshiluba dictionary making it English Kipendi. She also translated eighteen chapters of the Gospel of Matthew. She also had translated a catechism. April 30, 1924 Miss Sprunger came to Mukedi. Three weeks after she was there lightning struck the house and the translations burned except the dictionary which was in the store house.

At Mukedi the first whole book of the New Testament that was translated was Luke. On her second furlough it was printed by the British and Foreign Bible Society and the proof sheets were sent to her in the States. During the following term on the field all the books of the New Testament were translated. And this is the way it was done: a boy or young man that knew the Tshiluba language would read and translate into Kipende verse by verse. Before her were six or seven other versions, three English, the Authorized, Revised and Weymouth, one German, three French and sometimes also the Kikongo was consulted, although she did not know much about Kikongo. Whenever there was a question as to how a verse should be translated all the different versions were consulted, and usually the version that rendered itself most easily into Kipendi was chosen. Sometimes it was the German, sometimes one or the other of the French, sometimes Weymouth or one of the other English versions. Sometimes and more often than not, the version was chosen which agreed with the majority of the other versions.

The completed New Testament in the Kipende language was printed in 1934 by the British and Foreign Bible Society. By this time practically all of the Old Testament has been translated and is in use by the Sunday School and Day school. The Congo Inland Mission Board and the missionaries owe a large debt of gratitude to Miss Sprunger for the work she has done

"School buildings at the Mukedi Station, picture taken in 1941"

in translation.

In a discussion of the educational work of Mukedi station there are two things to be noted. First, the Belgium has launched a new educational program for the Congo. This program is to be carried out by the mission schools. This program of the state provides for nine years of education subdivided into three year periods. For the first three years little chapel schools are to be established in every tribal group with teachers that are qualified to teach the curriculum for the first three years. They shall receive the protection of the laws of Belgium. This gives the missionaries an opportunity not only to teach the elementary subjects but also the Word of God.

Second, that at the Mukedi station Rev. Vernon Sprunger received specialized training in Belgium to carry on the program stated above. The discussion of the educational problem has been kindly furnished by Rev. Sprunger. The first phase of the problem is the native population. The pupils come from an illiterate tribe. Before effective evangelism can be done the pupils must be taught to read. The natives themselves want education. As stated before, the call for teachers in the various villages is quite often a desire to be able to read as the white man does. The first problem the teacher faces is to make the school attractive for the children. These attractions must be of such a nature that they will not degrade the life of the pupil. The ideals of the Protestant schools are set high. It is more difficult to get the girls to school than the boys be-cause of the conception of womanhood that is held by the natives.

Another problem with the pupils is the curriculum. They all want arithmetic, reading and writing and French. They are not sure that they want very much writing. They see no sense in studying such things as general knowledge, nature, drawing, agriculture, lan-guage, etc. These subjects, however, are all on the state curriculum and so are included in our schools, as well as others not mentioned above. As is to be ex-pected the pupils do not apply themselves in the class-es that they do not care anything about, thus making teaching more difficult and the problem of the dis-cipline as well.

The native teachers themselves present a serious problem from the standpoint of educational standards. Not only do they not see the need of knowing methods of teaching but consider it an insult if the supervisor infers that they should learn how to teach. Then also in accordance with Bantu customs, the teachers believe that greatness comes in having many servants and having those servants work for you, rather than the Christian view of being a servant to all. The final problem stated by Mr. Sprunger is that of distinguishing between Belgian education and American. The Congo is a colony of Belgium and not of the United States. Missionaries sometimes find it difficult to adopt the Belgium methods of teaching. This is particularly noticed from the standpoint of methods of teaching as well as the nature of the curriculum. The missionaries must always remember that they are not sent to the Congo to make Americans but to lead the native to Christ so that he may become a native African Christian. All of this simply emphasizes the fact that more specialized training is needed by the missionaries in their various fields of service.

Education in the Congo is a much bigger job than it is in the United States of America. It is more difficult to raise the standard of an African from heathenism to a consecration to his God, than it is to teach a pupil from the first grade to completion of high school in America where religion does not enter into the field.

The final phase of work to be discussed in this chapter is that of the medical. In the thirty-five years

"A group of natives waiting for Medical care given them at the Dispensary"

of missionary work in the Congo by the Congo Inland Mission Board, only two doctors have been sent to the field. Before Rev. Haigh left in 1911 he pled with the board and the constituency for a young man to prepare himself as a doctor for our field. Up to 1931 our trained and practical nurses and even missionaries without medical training rendered a large service to the natives who were in need of medical help. The first doctor on the field was Dr. Rudolph Unruh. He was stationed at Mukedi but it was understood that he was to serve as the doctor for the four stations. The purpose of a doctor on the field was threefold. First to care for the health of the missionaries, second to treat the natives for disease and operations, and third, the creative task of teaching health and sanitation to the natives. The position and work of a doctor on the field is stated very clearly by the executive committee of the Congo Inland Mission Board when Dr. Unruh was sent over in 1931. As we are looking forward to the doctor's going to the field, the matter of the relation of the medical work to the mission as a whole and to the particular station at which the medical center is located, has been much in our minds. After carefully considering the matter we recommend that the following expression of position be sent to the field:

1. That we consider the medical work as an integral and essential part of the work and program of the mission as a whole, but that it is on the other hand, a distinctive work in its own field.

2. That in view of this fact we feel that since it requires a great deal of study and careful preparation for a doctor to qualify for his work, that by virtue of that training and experience, he should be accorded the privilege of formulating his own policy and program for the medical work and the methods of its promotion. We recognize the fact that under

such circumstances he may at times undertake to do things in a way which the more experienced missionaries would feel moved to disapprove or advise against; but we would urge that they be patient and let him try out the methods which he may choose, believing that if the attempt proves unfruitful, he will readily recognize the fact and revise his procedure accordingly. We assume, moreover, that the missionaries will stand ready at all times to give him the benefit of their experience when such council is solicited by him.

3. That we are confident that the doctor will manifest a real interest in the other and perhaps more distinctly spiritual phases of missionary work, but that as we know him we believe that he would find it more exacting to assume special or regular responsibility in those phases of the work than some others might. We feel that he should be given opportunity to serve in those capacities as he feels he can with ease, avoiding any undertaking which would burden him and result in a drain upon his energy which should be conserved for his special and exacting labors.

Dr. Unruh, after serving five years faithfully and efficiently, left on his furlough, March, 1936. He did not return to the field.

The field was again without a doctor until 1941, when Mr. Merle Schwartz had completed his training and was ready for the field. Dr. Schwartz, before he left for the field married Miss Dorothy Bowman, a trained nurse. They let on the ill-fated Zamzam and were held as prisoners for some time by the Germans. They sailed again in the fall of 1942 arriving at Mukedi, November 15, 1942. In the short time that they have been on the field they have visited all of the stations and report the health of the missionaries to be good.

Dr. Schwartz states that they could have two operations a day for an unlimited time without seeking out patients. The natives have money and come begging for operations but the need is supplies, medicine and help. The following report gives a review of their work of the day. Our usual hospital routine is something like this: At 6:15, after chapel in the church building, Merle meets with the hospital boys for their own morning devotions. Then begins the dispensary for mission people which is held first so that they can get to their work again. Then about 7:30 the village people come to the dispensary. When the crowd seems to be the largest the boys take turns in leading morning prayers with them. The reactions to the meeting, of the natives, are many but we know that God's Word will not return unto Him void. Medicines are given and the charts written and filed by two boys while another is doing microscopic work and another is out washing and dressing the tropical ulcers. Medical work in Congo is extremely interesting for we see many things that are uncommon at home. How discouraging to see patients with diseases for which there are no known treatment or cure. But how glorious to be able to give them a message of hope for eternal salvation even if the physical body cannot be cured.

Number of missionaries on the station, 8; number of church members at the end of 1944, 336; converts awaiting baptism, 3062; number attending Sunday morning services, 730; Sunday School, 703; prayer meeting, 220; Christian Endeavor, 402; number enrolled in Bible training school, 16; natives at the stations, 154; number of regional schools, 4; rural schools, 32; number of teachers regional schools, 15; number of teachers rural schools, 33; the primary school attendance, 367; regional schools, 209; rural schools, 363; native medical helpers, 7; number of patients treated, 4377; microscopic examinations, 2777; number of acres cultivated, 45.

The following missionaries have served at the Mukedi station: Miss Agnes Sprunger 1924-1945, Miss Amelia Bertsche 1928-1931, Miss Alma Doering 1923-1925, Mosers 1923-1945, Miss Erma Birkey 1923-1945, Sprungers 1931-1945, Dr. Rudolph Unruh 1931-1936, Dr. and Mrs. Merle Schwartz 1942-1945.

CHAPTER XV

# The Congo Inland Mission

## A CO-OPERATIVE PROGRAM

The history of the work of the Congo Inland Mission reveals continually its spirit of co-operation. This co-operation is manifested both on the field and in the home land as will be illustrated by this chapter.

The first expression of co-operation is in the organization of the Congo Inland Mission Board. Representatives from the Defenseless Conference and Central Conference of Mennonites organized the United Mennonite Board of Missions on March 22, 1911, which on January 23, 1912 became the Congo Inland Mission Board. This Board has had only three presidents in the thirty-five years of its history. The first was Rev. Valentine Strubhar 1911-1925, the sceond was Rev. Emanuel Slagle 1920-1934, the third Albert Neuenschwander 1934-1945 who is at present our very efficient president. The secretary-treasurers of the Board were as follows: D. N. Claudon 1911-1926, Rev. I. R. Detweiler 1926-1934, Rev. A. M. Eash secretary 1928-1936 and treasurer 1934-1936, Rev. C. E. Rediger is at present our capable secretary-treasurer 1936-1945.

The second co-operative part of our program is the Ladies Auxiliary. From the days of Paul down to the present time a great deal of commendation and credit must be given to the women of the Church. Their deep interest and great faith and expression in their activities have meant much in the missionary cause. Their work as missionaries on the field and co-operative effort in the home land exemplify steadfast faith and unselfish devotion and service.

The history of Ladies Aid Societies is linked very closely to the history of missions in both conferences. In the Central Conference of Mennonites Ladies' Aid Societies began when the first home mission was established in Chicago in 1909. The Defenseless Conference Ladies' Aid Societies were formed as early as 1900. After the beginning of the Congo Inland Mission work in 1911 the ladies of the congregations sent clothing and money to the field. Mrs. C. R. Egle and Mrs. Andrew Vercler were appointed by the Congo Inland Mission Board to have charge of this work. In 1925 the Ladies Aid Societies of the congregations of Central Conference united in a Conference Ladies Aid that they might do more systematic and effective work in missions both in the home and foreign field.

After the visit of the Field Secretary, Rev. Eash, to the Congo, the ladies were encouraged to form a united organization to help in clothing the native children in Africa. The Field Committee and the Annual Meeting held at Mukedi in 1929 recommended such an organization. The matter was presented to the ladies of the Defenseless and Central Conferences on October 24, 1929 at Bloomington, Illinois with forty-six ladies participating. After a general discussion at this meeting a motion was made by Mrs. Wm. B. Weaver, seconded by Mrs. M. L. Ramseyer that such a united organization be formed and that it assumes the responsibility of furnishing the clothing for all the station children of the mission. This was unanimously accepted. The ladies definitely stated that the purpose of the organization should be to assist the Mission Board wherever possible and relieve the Board of the responsibility and costs of supplying the clothing for the mission boys and girls. The officers of the first organization were as follows: president, Mrs. S. E. Maurer; vice president, Mrs. Elmer Stuckey; secretary,

Mrs. N. A. Goldsmith. At the same time a letter was sent to the field informing the missionaries of what was done and assuring them of the ladies' willingness to co-operate with them. They also asked for such information as the missionaries thought would be beneficial.

Since that time the Ladies Auxiliary has been in constant touch with the field both through correspondence and through the missionary ladies who come home on their furloughs. In 1937 it was felt wise to send only the cloth to the field and ask that the natives should be allowed to do their own sewing, since the missionaries had been teaching the natives sewing as a part of their educational program. After the forming of this united organization the Defenseless congregations organized Ladies Aid Societies. The same thing was true of the Evangelical Mennonites until today the three Mennonite groups of ladies are co-operating in this great project.

A few reports will reveal the progress the ladies have made in their co-operative effort. Once a year at the semi-annual meeting of the Congo Inland Mission Board the Ladies Auxiliary representatives meet with the Board. The following report was given in the October 13, 1942 meeting. In the report of the work of the Ladies Auxiliary, Mrs. N. J. Schmucker reported that the ladies of the Defenseless Conference had met in full their portion of the budget for clothing for station boys and girls ($350) and in addition had contributed over $300 for the passage for Mrs. Schwartz. Mrs. Stahly reported that the ladies of the Central Conference had met their portion of the budget for clothing ($700) and had made an additional contribution to Mrs. Schwartz's passage: and that the ladies of the Evangelical Conference had more than provided for the clothing for Nyanga station. The report was accepted with the thanks of the Board for the service rendered. The ladies further reported following their separate session that they adopted a budget of $1400 for the next year. It might be noted here that the young people of the Defenseless Conference furnished part support for Mrs. Schwartz while the Christian Endeavor Union of the Central Conference supported Dr. Schwartz.

In the meeting of the Congo Inland Mission Board of October 12, 1943 the ladies gave the following report: contributed for clothing $1443.67; special projects and medical shares $505; Mrs. Schwartz's passage $434; special gifts $320 and the following articles made and sent to the field: 36 sheets, 38 pillow slips; 44 baby layettes; 10 blankets; 11 boys' shirts; 27 dresses; 160 pounds of bandage material. The report was accepted with thanks for the service rendered.

The final report given at this year's meeting of the Board, October 10, 1944 is as follows: The Ladies Auxiliary reported on work done during the past year and plans for the coming year. The total value of contributions in cash sent to the field amounted to $3,010.-96. Plans for the coming year are: for clothing, Central Conference $700. Defenseless Conference $350. Evangelical Conference $350. Each local society is to be encouraged to assume a medical share. They will also endeavor to provide hospital supplies as heretofore, and recommend that at the next conferences a Ladies Auxiliary building fund be set up to provide for necessary missionary dwellings on the field.

These reports and brief history of the Ladies Auxiliary reveals the marvelous work which is being done by the ladies of our churches. There is yet one practically untouched field in which the ladies could co-operate with the missionary ladies on the field and that is in baby welfare work as begun at Mukedi and in better Christian homes among the native Christians.

This co-operative work of the Ladies Auxiliary challenges the women of our churches to an even larger and more efficient service for the native Christian Church and the Kingdom of God.

The second co-operative activity in the Congo Inland Mission work is that of other Mennonite groups. From the beginning of our work there has been close contact between the Conference of the Evangelical Mennonite Brethren and the Congo Inland Mission Board. In 1910 representatives from the Central Conference and of the Defenseless Conference attended the Evangelical Brethren's Conference at Mountain Lake, Minnesota. A number of their brethren attended our conferences throughout 1909-1912. The Congo Inland Mission Board has sent missionaries from this group to the field. In 1938 the Evangelical Mennonite Brethren sent an official representative to be a member of the Congo Inland Mission Board. This representative is now (1945) Rev. H. H. Dick of Dallas, Oregon, secretary of their Home and Foreign Mission Board. Rev. Dick's presence on the Board has been of great help in the inspiration he gives and his counsel in matters concerning our work on the field.

Another expression of co-operation is the plan worked out by the General Conference of Mennonites of North America and the Congo Inland Mission Board. In the Foreign Mission Board meeting of the General Conference held at Newton, Kansas, February 17-19, 1943 one of the main problems discussed was that of finding the best new open doors for missions to take the place of those which were closed in China. The field of Africa was given serious consideration. There were a number of young people in the General Conference who, as candidates for mission work, were interested in the Congo field. On the other hand, representatives of the Foreign Board had met with the Congo Inland

Mission Board a number of times to make friendly contacts between the various groups looking towards co-operative action. On October 13, 1942 at the Congo Inland Mission Board meeting Rev. P. H. Rickert presented the interest of his Board in closer co-operation with this Board in our Congo work, in view of the fact that they frequently have missionary candidates who wish to go to Africa, and with conditions becoming more and more averse to work in China, they need a new outlet for missionary activity in foreign lands. The question was raised of what sort of reciprocal relation might best be affected as an initial step toward such co-operative arrangement. A motion was made at this same Board meeting that our Field Secretary, Rev. Rediger, should attend the Mission Board meeting of the General Conference. In the Board meeting of April 8, 1943, Rev. Rediger gave his report which resulted in a motion that our executive committee meet with their executive committee to work out the agreement.

The next step was the meeting of the executive committee of the Congo Inland Mission Board and the executive committee of the Foreign Board in Chicago in May, 1943. The secretary of the Foreign Board of General Conference expressed their interest in this co-operative venture in the following statement: "Our Board was induced to take this step on account of a number of workers who have already been lost to our work and serve under other boards, although their support comes largely or entirely from our conference churches. This does not make for unity in our conference. If ever we need unity among ourselves, it is in times like these when the very existence of our distinctive doctrines is at stake. So we have already accepted a few candidates for Africa to go there as soon as they are ready and passage can be secured. For this new venture we also need the prayers of our mission friends."

After several meetings by representatives of the General Conference and the Congo Inland Mission Board the following plan for co-operation in doing mission work in the Congo was accepted by both organizations. In these resolutions C. I. M. stands for Congo Inland Mission and G. C. M. C. for General Conference of the Mennonite Church of North America.

## PLAN FOR CO-OPERATION IN DOING MISSION WORK IN AFRICA

1. The Board of Foreign Missions of the G. C. M. C. gratefully accepts the offer of the C. I. M. Board, according to which missionaries appointed for work in Africa by the former Board can be sent out co-operatively with the latter Board to work on stations of the C. I. M. Board in the Belgian Congo.

2. The Board of Foreign Missions of the G. C. M. C. offers to the C. I. M. Board a similar arrangement, so that if the latter Board desires to send missionaries into countries where the G. C. M. C. is engaged in mission work, these missionaries can be sent out co-operatively to work on the stations of the G. C. M. C.

3. No one shall be sent out as a missionary under this co-operative plan unless the candidate has been examined and approved by both of the co-operating Boards.

4. Missionaries that are sent out under this plan shall send a copy of their reports to both of the co-operating Boards, so that both Boards at all times will be informed about the work and its needs and problems. The administrative authority, however, is to remain at all times in the hands of the Conference (Board) which has charge of that mission field.

5. Salaries (allowances), outfit allowances, travel expenses for missionaries appointed for Africa by the

Board of Foreign Missions of the G. C. M. C. will be paid from the treasury of said Board. The money will be sent to the C. I. M. Board for remittance. The amounts paid shall be the same as those paid by the C. I. M. Board to their missionaries. Station budget money should be handled the same way; the amount to be paid shall be determined by the co-operating Boards.

This arrangement shall also hold for missionaries sent by the C. I. M. Board to fields of the G. C. M. C., so that in such a case the C. I. M. Board will pay allowances, etc., for the missionaries appointed by this Board.

6. No attempt shall be made by the Board of Foreign Missions of the G. C. M. C. to solicit money in the churches of the conferences of the C. I. M. neither for special projects nor for general mission purposes to be used in its mission fields unless such permission has been granted by these Conferences, nor shall the C. I. M. solicit money in the churches of the G. C. M. C. unless such permission has been granted by its Board of Foreign Missions.

7. Missionaries on furlough shall be under the supervision of the Board that pays its salaries (allowances). The two Boards shall, however, consult with each other to agree as to the furlough program of the missionary. As much as possible he shall visit and report on the work not only in the conference churches that supply the allowances, but also in the other co-operating conferences.

In addition to the groups that are directly affiliated from the standpoint of the Board there are six Mennonite groups represented by the missionaries on the field. These groups are, Defenseless Mennonite Conference; Central Conference of Mennonites; The Evangelical Mennonite Brethren; General Conference of Mennonites; Missionary Church Association and Bethel

Church of Inman, Kansas.

One of the very effective activities of the Congo Inland Mission Board is the giving of information and the creating of interest through literature. This information from 1910-1923 was given through the Christian Evangel and Zion's Tidings. These served as main sources for this history up to 1923. In this year the Congo Inland Mission Quarterly was issued. This was largely due to the fact that the Grand Rapids Auxiliary joined the Congo Inland Mission Board and that their constituency was eager for information concerning the mission work in the Congo. This small magazine was issued from 1923-1926. In this year, after Rev. I. R. Detweiler became the secretary-treasurer, missionary bulletins were issued. This continued until 1929 when the Congo Missionary Messenger was published. Its first issue was in August and is still being published. This magazine has been a real messenger in presenting the work on the field and the problems of missionary work both from the viewpoint of the home, the constituency and the field. Letters of missionaries which otherwise would have practically no circulation became the common property of all the readers of the Congo Missionary Messenger. The encouragement of certain missionary plans and projects find their place in this paper. Finally, the purpose of the writing of the "Twenty-five Years of Missionary Work in the Congo" by Rev. Harry Bertsche and the writer published in 1938 added to the fund of information concerning the field. The matter of writing a history of the Congo Inland Mission work had been a matter of discussion in the Board for five years. In the Congo Inland Mission Board meeting, April 11, 1939 a motion was made that the executive committee takes steps looking towards the publication of a more complete history of the Congo Inland Mission. After the present writer was appointed he began to gather material both from the field and home sources and now in 1945 is presenting this history as a further source of information concerning the field. It is the hope of the author that it might make its contribution both to the missionaries as well as to the Board and the Constituency.

There are a few co-operative activities from the standpoint of the field which should be discussed briefly in the close of this chapter. In the first place we should be finally reminded again of the very valuable contribution made by the co-operative spirit of the Southern Presbyterians all through the history of our mission work. The help given through them in languages, literature and medical aid can not be estimated materially. There are of course, other neighboring missions that have been friendly and co-operative.

The Congo Protestant Council or C. P. C., has been of great help to our work on the field. The publication of the Congo Mission News 1912-1945 gives information of the work of the thirty some missionary societies in the Congo. Then the supervision and visitation of the secretary of the Council has been very valuable. The very able leadership of Dr. Emory Ross for over fifteen years secretary of the Council has contributed much to the success of our work on the field as well as the information given to the home board in his visits to America. Another co-operative effort in the Congo was the building of the Union House at Leopoldville in 1920. The missionary societies in the Congo support this institution. Its purpose is to furnish the missionaries a Christian place for lodging and rest while coming and going to the field. This has been a great help to our missionaries when it becomes necessary to wait a considerable length of time on passage up the river or on the railroad. Because of the war conditions the missionaries have not been able to come home on their furloughs and so they have gone to the Andrew Murray Rest Home and other homes in Cape Town, Southern Africa. Another rest home was built through a gift of $3,000 by a lady in one of the Defense-less congregations. This rest home was built under the superision of Rev. Moser thirty-five miles north and west of Charlesville by Lake Madimape. This furnishes temporary rest to our missionaries for ten days or a month at a time.

The Congo Inland Mission Board is deeply grateful to all of these groups, organizations and activities that have meant so much to the progress of our work in these thirty-five years. Our appreciation can be expressed best by a larger and more efficient service in the salvation of souls and in the building of an African Christian Church.

## CHAPTER XVI

# "What Hath God Wrought"

As we come to the closing chapter in this history and look back over the work that has been accomplished through the guidance of the Holy Spirit, we are prompted to repeat the message which was given over the first cable laid from England to the United States, "What hath God wrought." This missionary work was done through years of tremendous changes in the Congo, educationally, economically and spiritually. These changes cannot onl ybe seen in civilization but in missionary work as well. The personnel on the Board changed; some missionaries left the field and others came; great changes occurred in the Church; missionary methods changed; even the attitude of the natives changed tremendously. The problems on the field have changed continually and with it all, the opportunities changed from time to time. But in the midst of the changing scenes there are those things that abide. God never changes; Christ never changes; the human soul never changes except as it is reborn through Christ; the Gospel has not changed; our faith has not changed; the great purpose of missions has been unchanged; finally, moral and spiritual realities are unchanging.

These changes were not all barriers to mission work. Some came as a result of the progress of the work. Even those that became obstacles brought a challenge to the missionaries. The changes which we wish to see are those mentioned by an elderly missionary in another society when he says, "As a result of missionary work there are Christian churches in every part of Belgian Congo, a large number of them being self supporting, self propagating, self governing indigenous churches with schools from the common bush school to schools for the preparation of teachers and preachers to carry on the work."

In its outpouring of life and treasure, usually unselfish and voluntary, the Christian Foreign Missions the last one hundred and fifty years are unequalled in magnitude by any other religious movement in the history of the world. Tens of thousands of men and women have given their lives as missionaries, gone to the jungles of Africa, braved ill health, dangers, persecution, misunderstanding, separation of families, mastered alien languages, translated it, had uncomfortable methods of living with no thought of personal gain. Millions of dollars were given by millions of Christians for people they never saw.

The facts narrated in this book are a sufficient defense of the claim that the contribution made by missions to the extension of civilization in the Congo can not be ignored. It is of supreme importance to the welfare of the whole of Africa that so centrally situated and so vast a colony as the Belgian Congo should ultimately become a Christian country whose native population will measure its standards of individual, civic and social conduct by the law of Christ. The forces which mold the life of the modern African are so powerful, the changes that take place around him are so kaleidoscopic, and the temptations and attractions that reach him are so various, that only those who have been transformed in their minds to "prove what is that good, and acceptable, and perfect will of God" will be able to preserve a full degree of integrity and freedom.

It is no small part of the contribution of missions that, through their agencies, education, medical facilities, and often social services have come to the African, not as the gift or byproduct of the highly organized modern state, but as prompted and inspired by the appeal of the Christian Gospel. The original motive of these social services, and the true source of their existence, are made clear through their connection with the work of Christian mission. No more valuable course could have been followed in order to guard the coming generation of Africans, in so far as may be possible, from a widespread secularization of life and a degradation of their civilization.

Concerning the changes that have taken place in missions in the last twenty-five years, Dr. Davis of the Bolenge Missions says, "It has been stimulating to watch the changes that have taken place in the years that I spent there. There is coming to be a new under-standing of the task that is before them. It used to be the white man's church and the white man's religion and the white man's Christ. Now the natives are think-ing of these as their own. They are beginning to real-ize that the responsibility for the coming of the King-dom in Congo is their own. They are beginning to stand on their own feet. It is vital and promising shift of attitude. It is as if they had at last crossed the swamp with its muds and pitfalls and were starting up the hill on the other side.

These are days when it seems to be popular to be-little the missionary and the missionary activity of the church, but I am proud to have been associated with the missionary venture and with those who are engag-ed in it. I feel that I have gotten large returns from my investment in the Congo. To have set a bone and pulled a tooth; to have removed a tumor and given an injection of Neosalvarsan; to have healed the sores of the leper and saved the life of a starving baby in the situation where they would otherwise have gone un-treated—those things will compensate for much I may have missed. To have been a friend to those who had few friends (whose very language had no word for friend) and to have relieved the stifling fears of many by teaching them of Him whose love casteth out fear—that is, to me, an adequate apologetic for the cause.

No one who has witnessed the changes of the past few years could doubt the value of his support to such a cause.

We are more firmly convinced than ever before that the gospel of the Lord Jesus Christ is the **one and only hope of mankind.** The fundamental missionary motives are eternal and unchanging. As long as the curse of sin and death holds the race in bondage, just so long will the good news of salvation be imperatively necessary for the redemption and restoration of a fallen race. Man's **need** for a Saviour from sin has not changed; God's **love** of the sinner has not changed; and Christ's **power** and will to save has not changed. Everywhere in foreign lands, we have seen at close range the Gospel of the first century coming to grips with the degrading heathenism and unspeakable sin and moral leprosy of the twentieth century and everywhere we have seen the Gospel gloriously triumphant.

The motive and the imperative of the Christian missionary enterprise are eternal and unchanging. But **methods** of doing missionary work in all lands, and especially in the older mission fields, are changing rapidly. We are now passing through a very trying and critical transition period in mission work abroad; if we successfully pass this crisis, it is going to call for the most patient and sympathetic understanding and the most Christlike compassion on the part of our people in the homeland and especially of our missionaries on the foreign fields.

After all, missions continue to be a Christian movement and not merely a general humane endeavor. It is, to be sure, the most humane endeavor that humanity is now making, but it has its roots in something deeper than kindly impulses toward other people. There is no effective plea for missions which can be addressed to those who do not intend to be accounted Christians. If one really does not care greatly for Christ, he will not greatly care for Christ's call to service. One must "come" before one will "go." There is not enough "drive" in a mere humanitarian movement to carry one over seas on a mission for Christ, not to keep one there after the first shock of repulse by those whom one means to benefit. Nor is there sufficient force in the social impulse to persuade men in general to maintain persistent and sacrificial giving. The motives for such a work must be powerful and continuous, not intermittent and impulsive. The appeal has to be made to Christians, not to grownup Boy Scouts who are expected to do "a good deed every day," beautiful as that purpose is and fine as the habit is.

Today we recognize the newly arisen need in the world for a unifying and mollifying spirit. When nations and races were safely distant from each other, their underlying defects made little or no difference. Today, when nations and races are in unavoidable contact, there must be either conflict or understanding. Some form of brotherhood in the world must develop something that will make men everywhere try to understand each other and to work in fellowship. If it is asked whether there can be a brotherhood in the world, the reply is that there is one now—the Christian brotherhood. This is weak and ineffective in many places, betrayed over and over again by those who should be its staunchest supporters, but it is always present checking its own violations, challenging its membership to fuller sympathy, shaming them for their failures. It is no weak plea for missions that it is the largest single agency in forming this brotherhood, and that every rich man truly won to Christ automatically becomes a member of it.

Within the limits of this book we could not do more than give a brief sketch of the history of our work in the Congo. But this work demonstrates the power and guidance of the Divine Father who has watched over the developments of our work from the time it was conceived in prayer by brethren and sisters now passed to their reward, to the present time when the influence of our work is felt in the home land as well as in the Congo beyond the confines of our station. For our mission work began not as an organization or an institution, but as a vision and a conviction in the hearts of those who first sponsored it. Our danger today lies in the fact that we are sometimes prone to make primary, organizations, quotas, methods, which bury the spiritual impulse under the mass of machinery. When one looks back thirty-five years over the feeble beginnings and traces the lines of progress where there is a native Christian Church larger in membership than the combined membership of Defenseless and Central Conference. We would again say, What hath God wrought.

One of our missionaries reflecting on the life of the first missionary, whose grave can be seen from the mission, and the only adult missionary who died on the field in thirty-five years, he says, "As we sat in our study or as we walked upon the back veranda of our home in Congo, we could not help but see the grave of the first missionary of the Congo Inland Mission. Many times we could visualize those first missionaries as they pitched their tents in the large forests which once occupied the present site of the station, and the first tent was pitched only a few rods from our dwelling place near a large tree. Some years ago this large tree was destroyed, but in order to preserve memories, a new one of the same specie was planted in the roots of the old one and is sending its branches heavenward with the undaunting message of "Faith is the Victory." We can picture Mr. Stevenson in those early days of 1912 amidst trials and victories, headaches and heartaches, joys and sorrows, yet to his dying day in the year 1913, it was only Jesus that could break the chains of Satan and free those who were long bound in witchcraft and heathenism. Yet there were others to follow. How our hearts were touched when we heard of the death of Rev. Lester Bixel, who being seriously ill on the field, died in the home land, a true follower or soldier of the Cross. Then there is Mutombo Noah, an outstanding native who helped the veteran missionaries in opening up new stations, sticking to the last when all others failed them, yet was to die slowly with that dreadful disease of sleeping sickness. Have they failed in the Master's cause? No, for their motto to the end was, "For to me to live is Christ, and to die is gain."

Possibly never in the history of any of the present generation of Mennonites has such a revival and ingathering of souls into the kingdom occurred within our ranks as has been going on in our mission in Africa in the past few years. In January, 1932, the Church in the mission numbered six hundred, and on January 1, 1934, it numbered over three thousand with another more than three thousand confessed believers who were receiving instruction prior to baptism. The Lord had in a marvelous manner shown His approval of the efforts put forth and used their feeble efforts to bring glory to His Holy Name.

As we come to the close of this history of our work in the Congo the question arises, what of the future? Is there still a need for missionaries in the Congo? What can be expected in the post war civilization in the

Congo? One of our leading statesmen has suggested the following developments which are sure to come as a result of this world revolution: 1. Belgium will retain Congo but grant more privileges to nations. 2. Increased education. 3. Increase campaign against diseases. 4. Develop consumer's goods. 5. Develop water power. 6. Conservation of forests. 7. Develop self government. 8. Some day perhaps develop an international administration of the Congo.

Some of the problems from the standpoint of missions will be the development of literature; co-operation with other missions; medical training schools; central training school and the development of African Christian leaders. Much of the leadership for the solution of these problems must come from the native Christian Church. Just as there was pioneering in the establishment of mission stations and the beginning of the work by white missionaries, the pioneering must now be done in the fields mentioned above. The pioneer's act is also unique: it can never be repeated. Some things can only be done once: Columbus discovered America and no one else can do it; Edison invented the phonograph and no one else can invent it. It is the privilege of the pioneer to do the unique act, which cannot be done a second time. It must further be our prayer that the "younger Churches" may have spiritual pioneers, men whose very presence in the congregation reveals the restlessness of a spiritual Alexander, ever sighing for new worlds to conquer. They must be men who can call the fainting back to God, who can inspire the Church, and declare the whole prupose of God in and through His people, who can freely face and accept responsibilty in a constant assurance of the love of God. Without such consecrated spiritual pioneers, we may well despair of the outcome of our missionary work.

Two of the outstanding world Christians and world missionary leaders are Dr. John R. Mott and Dr. Cornelius Patton. Dr. Mott visited the Congo in 1934 and held conferences with the missionaries. In these conferences he emphasized the following for a future African church: the growing indigenous church; larger evangelism; liberation of lay forces; application of the gospel to larger areas of life; and rapid progress in co-operative and practical Christianity. Dr. Patton in an address before the American Board of Missions set forth the following points for post war missions: 1. To transfer leadership to the national Christians. 2. To recognize more fully the responsibility of governments and to co-operate with them in so far as fundamental principles allow. 3. To apply Christianity in the environment in which the native is found. 4. Always to distinguish between Christianity and so-called Christian civilization. 5. To interpret the Christian message as it applies to the whole life. 6. To adapt education to the circumstances of a people and to furnish the background for the development of their Christian lives. 7. To work for the unity of the Christian missions on the field. 8. In the selection and training of missionaries to insist on the highest degree of efficiency. 9. To preach the eternal gospel by word and life so that the natives can understand. 10. To find in the leadership and saving power of Christ the only hope of a distressed and bewildered yet spiritually hungry world.

Christian teaching in Africa is almost all the teaching there is. At least eighty-five per cent of the total educational load in Africa is carried now by the Christian missions on that continent. Government in some instances subsidize, but it is the Christian force in Africa, foreign and African, which does almost all the African teaching. On no continent does distinctly Christian teaching carry so much of the load or have a greater opportunity. The greatest building, unifying, lifting force on the continent of Africa today is **Christian teaching.** And of the reflexes of that upon America and the world there can be no illusion. Tomorrow can be no different. Christian teaching forms Christian living. Christian living transforms the world.

With all of these tremendous changes taking place the question may arise, will there be any need for the white missionaries in the Congo in the future? One thing that has impressed us as we have studied the development and progress of our mission work is that these younger Christians and growing Churches greatly need the sympathetic understanding and loving counsel of the missionary. More than ever before, the missionary is needed for guidance and help in organizing the churches, in matters of self-government, of discipline and doctrine. If the missionary, like John the Baptist, is willing to "decrease" that the native churches and leaders may "increase" there is greater need for his services than ever before.

Also in the matter of training a native ministry and leadership, there is a greater need than ever. We can never send enough missionaries to evangelize all the nations. Our supreme task in the new epoch of missionary endeavor is to develop a native ministry that will evangelize its own land far better than we can. Therefore we are still going to need missionaries — many of them—to teach in schools, colleges, and seminaries; we will need missionary doctors and nurses; and men and women with gifts for writing, translating and creating worthy Christian literature.

The missionary of the future must be trained for leadership. He must be sound in body, have a good mind and adequately trained. It is sinful waste of money to send out a missionary who is unable or not interested in mastering the native tongue.

Most important of all, the new missionaries must be spiritually endowed. They must have the attitude of Jesus toward the lost and erring. If one has never been used to win souls to Christ in the home land, a mere change of residence to foreign land will not make them soul winners. One who goes as a missionary to a foreign land, should be able to say with Paul: "For I could wish that I myself were accursed for Christ for my brethren's sake, my kinsmen according to the flesh." The missionary must be one in spirit and purpose with Jesus in his statement, "For whosoever would save his life shall lose it; and whosoever shall lose his life for my sake and the gospel's shall save it."

A life yielded to God and controlled by His Spirit. A restful trust in God for the supply of all needs. A sympathetic spirit and a willingness to take a lowly place. Tact in dealing with men and adaptability toward circumstances. Zeal in service and steadfastness in discouragement. Love for communion with God and for the study of His Word. Some experience and blessing in the Lord's work at home. These are the qualities of an efficient missionary. All good work has its adversaries, so have missions.

But the greatest "adversary" to missions, the only one we really need fear, is the hindrance we ourselves can be through thoughtlessness and neglect. Opposition from without, our missionaries expect; indifference within the Church all but breaks their hearts. The test of carrying on with inadequate support, unable to touch the needs around them, and wondering whether the Church has forgotten, brings them their sorest trial. They return on furlough and find us living in elegant homes. They see our streets choked with shining cars. They watch the throngs that jam our athletic fields, and reflect that the price of one football ticket would  pay the salary of a native evangelist in Africa for two months. They read that a thrill-crazed crowd has paid in one night to see a prize fight more than the whole Church ever gave in a year to foreign missions. They wonder if Christ has lost first place in the hearts of American Christians.

How mighty have been the triumphs of the gospel in the Congo. Were it within the bounds of this history, how a person would enjoy the privilege of recounting the many wonderful victories wrought through the preaching of the Gospel of the Son of God! Handicaps? Yes. Opposition? Yes. Victories? Multitudes! Perhaps these very things which we have numbered as hindrances to the progress of the Gospel have in reality been stepping stones to greater attainments than would otherwise have been possible.

As the Congo Inland Mission faces the new day that is coming to the Congo in the post war era, it feels that it should have first-hand information from the field as to what those changes will be. It is with this in mind that in the April, 1945 Board meeting the Board selected Rev. C. E. Rediger as its representative to visit the field. The prayers of the Board and the constituency go with him as he goes on this very important task. God loves the Congo, Jesus died for the Congo, the Holy Spirit works in the Congo; therefore there is and must be victory.

# Questionary

## Chapter I

1. What is the value of studying history?
2. How does the history of our work in Africa create greater interest?
3. What is the relation of the past to the present and future?
4. Give illustrations of where men and women became missionaries by reading biography.

## Chapter II

1. What is the relation of our conception of God to our missionary interest?
2. What is the real purpose of the missionary in going to the Congo?
3. Have an open discussion on why we have missions.
4. What is the relation between Christ's three great commandments? Come—Abide—Go.
5. Discuss love as a power.
6. Discuss the importance of the cross in our missionary thinking.
7. Write down seven reasons why you believe in missions.

## Chapter III

1. Why has Africa been called the Dark Continent?
2. Discuss the physical features of Africa as a continent.
3. Are its climate and the contour of the land conducive to exploration and missionary work?
4. What types of people ive in Africa?
5. How was the Congo River an aid to the opening of the territory?
6. Is it important for the missionary to study geo-

graphical conditions of the Congo?
7. Describe briefly some of the exploration.
8. How did Belgium get possession of the Congo.

### Chapter IV

1. What three qualifications are necessary for a skilled workman?
2. How does this apply to a missionary in the Congo?
3. Name six great resources of the Congo.
4. What are the outstanding characteristics of the Bantu people?
5. What is the importance of the missionary knowing the life of the native?
6. What changes have come about in the Congo in the last twenty-five years?
7. Have these changes helped or hindered the native in his life?
8. What are the two outstanding principles of the native's religion?
9. Is his religion a help or a hindrance to the acceptance of the gospel?

### Chapter V

1. Explain Livingstone's statement, "The end of exploration is the beginning of missionary enterprise."
2. Discuss the earliest missionary work done by Protestants in the Congo.
3. Give a brief history of the life of David Livingstone.
4. Name a few outstanding contributions he made to the opening of the Congo.
5. What further explorations were made by Stanley which aided in opening the Congo?

### Chapter VI

1. How did the work of Dr. Sheppard and Dr. Lapsley help us in the establishment of our work?

2. Discuss the work of Dr. William Sheppard.
3. What was the relation of the white people to the natives at this time?
4. Discuss the early missionary work in the Defenseless Conference of Mennonites.
5. Discuss the steps which led to the co-operative work of the Congo Inland Mission Board.
6. Why was the work discontinued in British East Africa?
7. Who were the persons largely responsible for the beginning of our work in the Congo?

### Chapter VII

1. Give a brief history of how the territory was selected which is now our field.
2. What reasons were given by Rev. Haigh and Rev. Stevenson for the selection of this field?
3. Name the men who were the first members of the Congo Inland Mission Board from the two co-operating groups.
4. How did the Southern Presbyterians help our missionaries in the establishment of our work?
5. Give a brief history of Rev. and Mrs. Haigh and Rev. A. J. Stevenson.
6. Tell what was done in the home church to acquaint the constituency with the new field.

### Chapter VIII

1. Describe the two visits made by Rev. and Mrs. Haigh to Kalamba.
2. Tell about the trip of Rev. Stevenson until he arrived at Kalamba.
3. What was the purpose of the tour by Stevenson and Haighs after his arrival?
4. What were the outstanding differences between Djoka Punda and Kalamba?
5. In what sense was this work pioneering?

6. Which station was established first, Kalamba or Djoka Punda?
7. When did the missionaries receive permission to make their work permanent at the two stations?
8. What new missionaries arrived in the beginning of 1912?
9. What was the effect of the death of Rev. Stevenson on the missionaries? On the constituency?
10. How many of our missionaries have died on the field?

### Chapter IX

1. What changes in the personnel of missionaries came about in 1916?
2. Give a brief review of the work as it was in 1916.
3. What phases of work were begun in these earlier years which are now being developed?
4. Give a brief history of the work of Rev. and Mrs. Haigh from 1911 to 1920.
5. Describe a typical Congo village.
6. What place do the villages hold in the program of mission work?
7. Describe the educational work done on both stations.
8. What missionaries are on the field by 1920?
9. Under whose leadership did the European missionaries come to the Congo field?
10. Why didn't the European missionaries stay?

### Chapter X

1. Give a brief history of the establishment of the Nyanga station. Of the Mukedi station.
2. In what tribe were these two stations established?
3. Discuss the changes that came about in the civilization of the Congo by 1925.
4. What reasons can you give for the sending of a representative to the field in 1928?

5. What was the result of this visit from the standpoint of the field?
6. What effect did it have on the constituency?
7. How was the Congo Missionary Messenger begun and why?

## Chapter XI

1. Review the history of the Charlesville station from 1912 to 1930.
2. Describe the tribes surrounding the station which needs to be evangelized.
3. What was the chief purpose in the establishment of this station?
4. What is the relation of Charlesville to the other three stations?
5. Tell the story of Songamadi.
6. What is the purpose of itinerating work?
7. Discuss briefly the different phases of work carried on at Charlesville now.
8. Study carefully the statistics at the close of this chapter.
9. Who are the present missionaries at Charlesville?

## Chapter XII

1. Give a brief review of the Kalamba station to 1930.
2. Is the Kalamba station located in the center of their work?
3. Discuss the report of the Kalamba station given by Rev. Barkman for 1931.
4. Discuss the evangelistic work of the Kalamba station.
5. What are the outstanding contributions made by Barkmans in their long term of service at Kalamba?
6. Describe the work that is done in music at this station.
7. Who are the present missionaries at Kalamba station?

### Chapter XIII

1. State the outstanding differences between the Baluba and Bampendi tribes.
2. Give a brief history of Nyanga until 1930.
3. Discuss the establishment of the first church at Nyanga.
4. Give a brief report of the industrial work that is done at this station.
5. What problems have the Nyanga missionaries faced in the development of their work?
6. What language needs to be used at the Nyanga station?
7. Tell about the girls' work at Nyanga.
8. What missionaries are now serving at the Nyanga station?

### Chapter XIV

1. Give a brief history of the Mukedi station from 1921 to 1930.
2. Discuss the location of this station.
3. Describe the translation work done by Miss Sprunger.
4. Describe the regional established on the stations.
5. Who was the first doctor sent to the Congo mission field?
6. Discuss the need for medical work in Congo.
7. Describe the work done by Dr. and Mrs. Merle Schwartz.
8. What is the relation of the educational work on the field to the educational system of Belgium?
9. Who were our earliest mssionaries on the Mukedi station?
10. Who are the present missionaries?

### Chapter XV

1. In what sense is the Congo Inland Mission work a co-operative effort?

2. Give a brief history of the work of the Ladies Auxillary.
3. What is the relation of the Congo Inland Mission Board to other Mennonite groups?
4. What are the sources for information of our work on the field?
5. State what could be done to bring about a closer contact with the missionaries on the field.
6. What agencies on the field have been of great help to our missionaries and to the work?

### Chapter XVI

1. State five definite goals to be attained in our missionary work in the Congo.
2. Describe briefly what God has wrought in the Congo.
3. What do we mean by the indigenuous church?
4. Is the work easier or more difficult today than in the early days?
5. What are some of the needs as we face the future in the Congo?
6. What is the significance of leadership for the future?
7. Name some of the outstanding post war problems.
8. Compare and contrast the adversaries with the triumph of the gospel in the Congo.

# Bibliography

## I. Source Material

1. Annual letters from the field.
2. Annual reports of Mission Board.
3. Christian Evangel. July, 1910—May, 1945.
4. Congo Mission Board Secretary Report.
5. Congo Missionary Messenger. August, 1929—May, 1945.
6. Congo Mission News. 1928—1930.
7. Congo Inland Mission Quarterly. 1921—1924.
8. Field Secretary Reports.
9. Field Station and Statistical Reports.
10. Heilsbote. 1912—1916.
11. Personal Correspondence.
12. Twenty-five Years of Mission Work in the Congo.
13. Year Books. 1921—1945.
14. Zion's Tidings. 1924—1945.

## II. Secondary Material

1. Europe since 1815. Hazen.
2. History of the Christian Church. Walker.
3. Livingstone the Pathfinder. Basil Mathews.
4. David Livingstone. Campbell.
5. African Ways and Wisdom. T. Cullen Young.
6. African Beliefs and Christian Faith. Edwin Smith.
7. Thinking with Africa. Milton Stauffer.
8. Out of Africa. Emory Ross.
9. The Lure of Africa. Cornelius Patton.
10. The New Africa. Donald Fraser.
11. The Missionary Imperative. Clark.
12. The New Map of Africa. Gibbons.
13. The Soul of the Bantu. Willoughby.

14. Nature Worship and Taboo. Willoughby.
15. Centennial History of the Mennonites of Illinois. Harry F. Weber.
16. Central Conference of Mennonites. William B. Weaver.
17. Missionary Review Magazine. 1908—1930.
18. The Church in History. Nagler.

# Members of the Congo Inland Mission Board from 1911-1945 and terms of service

Valentine Strubhar 1911-1926
C. R. Egle 1911-1926
J. H. King 1911-1926
Benjamin Rupp 1911-1925
J. K. Gerig 1911-1924; 1925-1929
Peter Schantz 1911-1922
Aaron Augspurger 1911-1917; 1922-1928
    (Honorary)
D. N. Claudon 1911-1926
Emanuel Troyer 1917-1942
Emanuel Slagle 1917-1943
S. E. Maurer 1925-1933
Noah Goldsmith 1925-1928
I. R. Detweiler 1926-1943
E. J. Oyer 1925-1934
Jacob Schmucker 1925-1928
    (Honorary)
Ben Rediger 1925-1928
Wm. B. Weaver 1926-1945
Allen Yoder 1928-1945
A. M. Eash 1928-1936
C. E. Rediger 1928-1933; 1936-1945
H. E. Bertsche 1928-1945
Amos Oyer 1928-1931
Noah Schmucker 1929-1931
G. P. Schultz 1928-1933; 1937-1940
B. F. Leightner 1928-1929
H. H. D. Langeria 1921-1925; 1928-1933
P. L. Eicher 1929-1931
Albert Neuenschwander 1931-1945

Elmer Stuckey 1931-1936
Emanuel Rocke 1933-1945
N. O. Hoover 1933-1945
A. F. Weins 1933-1935
George Fast 1933-1935
J. P. Barkman 1934-1935
J. N. Schmucker 1935-1945
R. L. Hartzler 1937-1945
H. P. Fast 1940-1941
H. H. Dick 1941-1945
George Gundy 1942-1945
Reuben Short 1943-1945
Wilmer Shelly 1943-1944
Alvin Beachy 1944-1945
A. E. Kreider 1945—

## In Memoriam
John 4:38. Others labored.

### MISSIONARIES
Alvin J. Stevenson, Feb. 1913
Lester Bixel, July 1934

### BOARD MEMBERS
Valentine Strubhar, July 1941
C. R. Egle, June 1926
J. H. King, March 1935
Benjamin Rupp, May 1929
J. K. Gerig, April 7, 1944
Peter Schantz, July 1925
Emanuel Troyer, June 1942
Emanuel Slagle, June 1944
Jacob Schmucker, October 1942
Amos Oyer, December 1931
Elmer Stuckey, March 1939
A. F. Weins, January 10, 1937